# INVERNESS REMEMBERED
# VII

*Published By*
New Century Publishing Group

**New Century**
Publishing Group

# INVERNESS REMEMBERED VII

## VII

### Edited and Compiled by Willie Morrison

CONTRIBUTORS

Mrs Sheila Burnett

Mrs Joan Clyne

Chalmers Proudfoot

Philip Owen

Mrs Joyce R MacKenzie

Alan MacLeod

Mrs Marjory Walker

Alan Miller

Gordon Gilliespie

Stewart MacLennan

Murdo MacKenzie

Mrs Rose Ann MacKenzie

Jamie Angus

Duncan Mackintosh

Allan Cameron

Mrs Ishbel MacQueen

Mrs Eileen MacKinnon

Mrs Raye Leith

William F MacDonald

Mrs Sandra Wilson

Alan and Sheila Simmons

Mrs Marjory Dunn

Mr and Mrs D Robertson

Ms Kate Cumming

D MacDonald

Mrs Wilma MacKenzie

James MacKenzie

Archie Burns

Ms Sandie MacKenzie

Mrs Dorothy Ahearn

Alex Grant

Alistair MacDonald

John Hay

Mrs Elizabeth Fraser

Mrs Mary Wylie

Ms Sue Owen

Marjorie Stuart,

M Nicoll,

Jeff MacLeod,

Duncan and Marjorie Robertson

Duncan Mackay

Mrs Daphne Campbell

Brian Corbett

Fred Millwood

Mrs Eileen Foster

Mrs Margaret E MacDonald

Hamish Gordon

George Maclean

Mrs Kathleen Kesson

Mrs Helyn Wilson

Mrs P Cook

Copyright 2011

ALL RIGHTS RESERVED

No part of this publication may be reproduced, stored in a retrieval system, or transmitted in any form or by any means, electronic, electrostatic, magnetic tape, mechanical photocopying, recording or otherwise, without permission in writing from the publishers.

A Catalogue Record for this book is available from The British Library.

# CONTENTS

# INTRODUCTION

ANOTHER year has flown by all too swiftly and once again we present the latest volume of Inverness Remembered.

As in previous issues, the photographs from Inverness and district in this volume cover many decades, from beyond living memory to events still well remembered by those of a certain age.

Once again the primary aim is to record examples of how ordinary people of yesteryear lived, learned, worked and enjoyed themselves.

While it is inevitable that photos of celebrities or members of the national and local great and good appear on our pages, by far the majority of people pictured belong to the modest majority, who went about their business day after day, year after year, with minimum fuss and often little recognition.

However, a few recollections have come to light of some local folk of yore, in their time well-known, now sadly almost forgotten, but worthy of remembrance for their contributions to the life of our city and its environs.

It's amazing how each year, so far, local folk and exiles have revisited their own or their ancestral pasts, and have emerged not only with so many intriguing photos, but also with interesting anecdotes or potted biographies to accompany them.

We give heartfelt thanks to all our contributors, including those who have contacted us to comment on or to correct captions for photos from earlier issues.

## APOLOGY

And now for an apology, to those contributors whose photos have not appeared this year. Inverness Remembered has become almost a victim of its own success, to the extent that last year we were left with many more photos than we could use, so quite fairly we gave these priority in this year's issue.

The same has happened again in Inverness Remembered VII, with the result that a great many contributors' pictures are not featured here. We have tended to process photos on a first-come basis, as we picked envelopes out of the huge pile of pictures received.

Be patient please. If your photos do not appear in Inverness Remembered VII, we will do our best to ensure that they appear in Inverness Remembered VIII, which we will already have started to work on, by the time this volume reaches the bookstalls.

We still have a large number of excellent photographs to provide a really good start to the next issue.

A word of advice to generous future contributors. While modern computer technology often allows us to improve old scratched or spotted photos - and we've included an example within of just what can be done in this respect - we are not normally able to reproduce photos from newspaper cuttings.

Finally, we hope we have again given you some worthwhile reading.

# Bygone Inverness

We have no specific information about the event depicted in this photo, but it seems to have been a ceremony to mark the arrival of a new fire engine in the burgh. The brass plaque on the apparatus states: "Merryweather & Sons, First Grand Fire Patent, Steam Fire Engine", one of thousands manufactured and exported all over the world in the 19th Century by a famous Greenwich company founded in 1836 by Moses Merryweather. The event must have taken place after the present Town House was completed in 1882. The bowler-hatted man with the large watch-chain fourth from the right may be town clerk Kenneth Macdonald, who held the post for 40 years, from 1881-1921.

A rare wartime photo taken around 1942, when film was scarce, at Drummondhill House, home of local businessman Frank Sime, pictured left in the rear row. With him, from left, are a Mrs Leask, from Edinburgh, his son-in-law, Dr Ian Macleod, Ian's daughter Sylvia, Gordon Lyon and his father Major Louis Lyon, who owned a sawmill at Carrbridge; front, from left: Jim Sime (sitting behind), his son Frank Sime, James Lyon, Alan Macleod, Stewart Sime, David Sime, Jeff Macleod and John Macleod, who later succeeded his father Aeneas as GP at Dornoch.

*This Inverness family photo from well over a century ago, submitted by Raye Leith, who thinks the lady holding the child is her great-grandmother Catherine Macleod, while she believes the lady standing next to her is her grandmother Margaret Macleod, who later married local man John Donaldson. The other two are possibly Catherine's other daughters Mary Macleod, later McIlwraith, and Ria. The picture was taken in Whyte's studio, 25 Bridge Street, Inverness.*

*A "before and after" study of two little girls of yesteryear, which demonstrates the computer's remarkable powers of photo enhancement. Raye Leith, who submitted it, thinks the little blonde girl may be her mother, Molly Donaldson, who lived at 7 Manse Place, Inverness, and the older girl her aunt Mina. "It's certainly Donaldson family, but I'm not certain," she admits. The remarkable transformation in the second photo was carried out by Inverness History Forum member, Inverness Remembered contributor and computer buff Allan Cameron, who says: "When I saw it, I couldn't resist the challenge."*

A childish scrawl on the back of this photo, by Andrew Paterson, of 15 Academy Street, Inverness, says "Dear Grann I hop you are..." There is also a more mature signature, "Donald Macleod". Raye Leith, who contributed it, believes the Edwardian lady is her great-grandmother Catherine Macleod.

An early photo, which seems to be the junction of Hamilton Street in the late 19th Century.

A formal photograph of the Fraser family, who lived at I High St, Clachnaharry, Inverness, taken around 1908. They are, from left: Harry, John, mother Mary Ann, father John Senior, Frederick, Donald, Elizabeth. John Fraser Snr was a mason. Mary Ann was a MacInnes from Drumbuie in Lochalsh. Freddie the youngest son, died tragically from appendicitis aged only 15, soon after this photo was taken. His father died very soon afterwards.

Duncan Dallas and his family, probably taken about 1908 outside their house at 42 Rose Street, Inverness. The trio at the rear, are, from left: John Dallas, father Duncan, Annie Dallas; front, from left: Helen Dallas Jnr, Duncan Dallas Jnr, mother Helen Dallas, with son Charlie on her knee, Mary and George Dallas. Duncan was a sawyer in the town. His eldest son John became a railway engine driver and lived at Lochcarron. George emigrated to New Zealand and had a family there. Charlie, the youngest, was killed in an accident in February 1960, during construction of the Ness Bridge. Jamie Angus, who is descended from Duncan Snr, through Annie, and who contributed this photo, says: "I believe he was crushed by some falling logs."

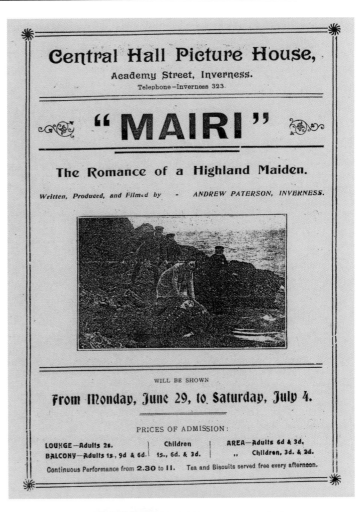

Central Hall Picture House,
Academy Street, Inverness.
Telephone—Inverness 323.

'Mairi' sub-titled 'The Romance of a Highland Maid', was one of the earliest story films made in Scotland, and certainly the earliest in the Highlands. Inverness photographer Andrew Paterson decided to use the coast near North Kessock as the setting for smuggling story with a love triangle and a happy ending. He wrote the script, directed and filmed the 17-minute mini-thriller, using eight local amateur actors. It was first shown at the Central Picture House in Academy Street on 20th May 1912 and was subsequently screened on several occasions. It was re-edited in 1953 by Playhouse Cinema manager and talented film-maker James Nairn, and is now preserved by the Scottish Screen Archive.

Members of Merkinch platoon of the Home Guard, proudly wearing the badge of the Queen's Own Cameron Highlanders on their headgear, are pictured here on parade in Portland Place. There is some suggestion that the picture might have been taken on the disbandment of the Home Guard in 1944, a few months before World War II ended, by which time all danger of invasion had long passed. The man eighth from the right in the front row is said to be a Mr McMahon, who owned a second-hand shop at 4 Grant Street. Many of these volunteers, unjustly mocked as "Dad's Army", would almost certainly have been veterans of the trenches in the Great War.

*Pipe Major Dan MacDonald, rear row, fourth from left, is pictured here in 1946, on the site where the Clach Social Club now stands, with his Army Cadet Force pipe band. How many members still survive?*

*This young lady, Elsie Mackintosh, nee Paterson, was pictured over a century ago with her rather fine roadster bicycle, on a personalised postcard of a kind then popular, addressed simply to Miss Paterson, Ballifeary House. The message on the postcard, postmarked at Inverness Post Office at 9.15am, on 1 May, 1905, states: "Dear B, I will be up to see you tonight. Hope you are well. Mother is feeling a little better today. She had a better night. E." Imagine expecting any item of correspondence to arrive at its destination on the same day in 2011!*

This 1920s study was snapped in the garden of the Free North Church Manse, Inverness, when the Rev John Macleod, pictured in front with his wife Margaret, was incumbent at the riverside church. Behind, from left, are members of their family, Alastair Macleod, Dr Isabel Macleod, Dr Ian Macleod, Mary Macleod, for many years a teacher at Central School, Inverness, and Dr Aeneas Macleod, who later served for long as GP at Dornoch. The former manse is now a nursing home, called Aden House.

The Free North Church Manse in Annfield Road, now Aden House Nursing Home, pictured between the wars, with minister, the Rev John Macleod, and his daughter Isabel at the front door. Isabel became a doctor in Inverness. Mr Macleod was later appointed principal of the Free Church College, Edinburgh.

*All we know about this interesting photo of a form of transport even then obsolescent is that it was taken on 24 July 1935 at Inverness Show.*

*According to a note on the back of the original, this photo was taken on 19 March 1939, in Muirtown Street, where the lady pictured, Anne Fraser, lived after moving from Bunchrew to help her daughter run her shop, after the death of the latter's husband.*

*Inverness teenager Tenby Fotheringham, pictured during an outing in the late 1930s to Nelson's Tower, Forres, with Jean Fraser, right, and her friend Hazel Allan.*

*This family picnic scene, with Anne Fraser, the old lady sitting in the middle, may have been snapped at Culloden Moor.*

*Widow Anne Fraser, at that time living at Muirtown Street, Inverness, is pictured here in 1937 with her grand-daughters Tenby and Voila Fotheringham.*

*John Fraser, like many young Inverness lads of pre-Great War years, occupied some of his leisure time and supplemented his income by enlisting in the Territorial Army, in his case the Lovat Scouts. When war came he was quickly involved in the bloodbath at Gallipoli, in the Dardanelles, fighting against the Turks. His family believe he was wounded at some point. Originally from Bunchrew, he survived the war, and worked for some years on the railway, living at 64 Ballifeary Road, Inverness, from 1930 for about 14 years. He then took over the tenancy of a farm at Grantown on Spey, where he spent the remainder of his life.*

Still going strong, three quarters of a century after first rolling off the production line at Longbridge, Birmingham - an Austin Ascot 1936 11.9 hp model, known as the 12/4 pictured at the annual Festival of Historic Transport, held at the Scottish Vintage Bus Museum, Lathalmond, Dunfermline, on 19 June 2011. Now owned by classic car enthusiast Eric Bowman, of Forfar, Angus, it was first registered on 31 Dec 1935 to Robert Bruce, of Kerrisdale, Muirfield Road, Inverness.

It's hard to believe that the man in the early 1950s picture, sitting on the Kessock Ferry passenger boat with his little daughter Elizabeth, is the same person as the baby in the rickshaw, drawn by a Japanese coolie in the next photo. Alistair Orient McLennan, for that was indeed his name, was born in 1908, in Kobe, Japan, where his father Duncan McLennan, an electrical engineer, worked for a number of years. His descendants believe he may have worked for the pioneering engineering genius Lord Kelvin. "My father was given Orient as his middle name because he was born in the east," says Elizabeth, now Fraser, who contributed these photos. Alistair, who subsequently enjoyed a long career with the Department of Agriculture, married an Ayrshire farmer's daughter called Roberta Barclay, and moved north when he inherited the family croft at Kilmuir Hill, near North Kessock, where Elizabeth and her three siblings were brought up. He died in 1987. His mother Jane was a Mackay from Lewis. Ironically Alistair's younger brother Duncan, a horticultural college lecturer, joined the RAF during World War II, became a prisoner-of-war of the Japanese, and was drowned with over 5,600 others, when the ship 'Junyo Maru', taking prisoners and slave labourers from Malaya to Sumatra, was torpedoed in September 1944 by the British submarine 'HMS Tradewind'.

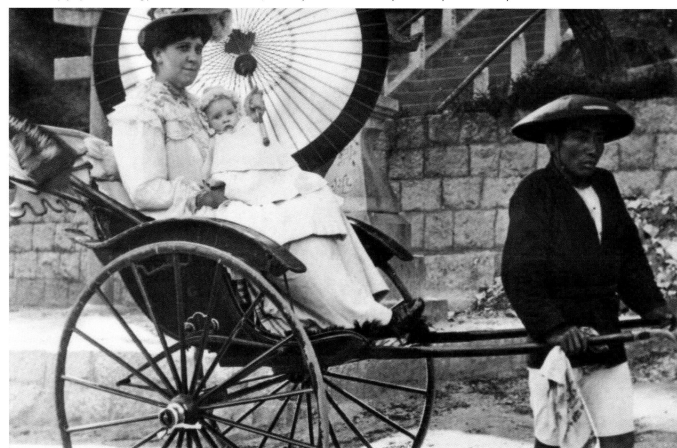

Call it as you like, collision or coalition of three languages, the modern community of Dalneigh is named after a mixture of Old Norse and Latinised Gaelic, 'Dail na Eich', or the dale of horses, with 'dal' a word introduced into the Highlands by Viking settlers of a millennium ago, and Gaelic each, the singular of horse, deriving from the Latin 'equus'. This was the long-demolished Dalneigh farmhouse as it looked around 90 years ago, shortly before the first council houses began to spring up on the farm's perimeter.

The venue is the main entrance to Ness Bank Church, still a thriving congregation, while the ladies are believed to be members of its Woman's Guild of over 70 years ago. The numerous fox-furs might be regarded as rather unpolitically-correct by members of today's congregation.

*Pictured here in the 1920s are eight members of the 10-strong Henderson family of Lynebeg Farm, Cawdor. Father George has Jean on his knee, while Mabel stands between him and her mother Ann. Second from the right, beside his big sister Annie is Bill, while behind are two older members, Geordie, left, and Sandy. Missing are Jonathan, who by that time had joined the Army as a boy soldier, and Robbie. Sadly all have now passed on.*

*From the age of the old car and the style of her clothes, this photo of Inverness lass Mabel Henderson in High Street must have been taken over 70 years ago. Her niece, Kathleen Kesson, thinks it dates from the late 1930s, by which time the car in the background, with the Aberdeen registration RG1683, would have been considerably older.*

# Businesses and workers

Members of National Union of Journalists Highland Branch welcome the union's Scottish regional organiser George Stone in the mid-1970s. With George and his many gifts ...re, from left: Alan Scott, David Love, Ron Lyon, Alan Dow, Nick Hunter, Alex Main, Stuart Lindsay, Neil MacPhail, Bill McAllister, Tommy Cameron and Reay Mackenzie.

Delegates to a National Bakers' Conference, featuring many members from Inverness. But where was the venue - certainly not the Old High Church, as has been suggested?

*Henderson's furniture store, owned by John Grant "Jock" Henderson, stood at the south end of Academy Street, next door to the Playhouse Cinema. The period can be fixed fairly precisely, as the Playhouse usually boasted an up-to-date programme, which you can just see, and its offerings for that particular date were The Storm, a thriller about a ship caught in a typhoon, starring Charles Bickford and Barton MacLane, and Service de Luxe, starring Constance Bennett, both released late in 1938. Henderson's went out of business in the mid-1940s.*

*When this photo was taken at the junction of Chapel Street and Waterloo Place around 1960, Inverness Farmers' Dairy still boasted at least one horse-drawn milk-float. Those of us of a certain age might recognise the car in the background, as a "new" Ford Anglia with a swept-back rear window, introduced in the autumn of 1959. Does anybody now remember who the milkman was, or what became of this fine fountain?*

## HIGHLAND DRESS

The healthiest, most sensible, and most romantic Dress for all. Gives a tone that no other garb can do. We specialise in

### KILT OUTFITS

*for*

LADIES, GENTS, BOYS, GIRLS

Give your Boy a Kilt. The Kilt Suit is most economical. You can rely on our Outfits as being correct.

ANY CLAN TARTAN SUPPLIED

Large selection of tartan souvenirs of every description always in stock including ties and scarves of every clan

## Wᵐ MACKENZIE

TARTAN SPECIALIST

## 11a BRIDGE ST INVERNESS

Phone: 891

*The youth pictured in this advert from the 'Book of Inverness' guidebook of 1939 seems just a trifle self-conscious modelling this "healthiest, most sensible and most romantic dress", which would today seem a little over-the-top even on a Highland dancer. How many readers remember tartan specialist William MacKenzie?*

---

## STRATHNESS Private Hotel :

Ideal situation on Banks of River Ness and Castle. Every Comfort and Convenience. H. and C. Electric Light. Terms Moderate.

• J. McEWAN, PROPRIETRIX •

### 4 ARDROSS TERRACE INVERNESS

PHONE 810

---

## Thomas Skinner

BAKER AND CONFECTIONER

BREAD AND CAKES SUPPLIED TO SHOOTING PARTIES

•

PICNICS AND PARTIES CATERED FOR ESTIMATES GIVEN FREE

•

WEDDING CAKES SUPPLIED AT SHORTEST NOTICE

## The Crown Bakery

2 STEPHEN'S BRAE ... INVERNESS

*Two more adverts from pre-war days, the lower featuring a popular bakery which soldiered on until the 1970s.*

---

# FURNITURE

We are Manufacturers of High Grade Furniture, and hold large stocks suitable for Dining-Rooms, Lounge and Bedrooms, which we can offer at Keenest Prices.

## Carpets and Linoleums

We invite inspection of our large range of Seamless Axminster and Wilton Squares, Oriental Carpets, etc. which is the largest in the North of Scotland.

:-: Inlaid and Printed Linoleums at Best Prices :-:

*Removals Contractors and Auctioneers*

INVENTORIES AND VALUATIONS CAREFULLY MADE UP

## MACIVER & CO.

64-68 Church St. and 45-49 Academy St.

### INVERNESS

Telegrams: "Maciver's, Upholsterers, Inverness"
Telephone: Inverness **46**

*Another name featured in the 'Book of Inverness', not so long vanished from Academy Street is MacIver & Co.*

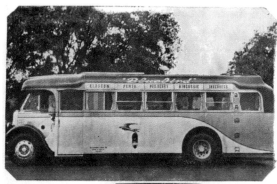

**T**HESE illustrations show you the handsome exterior of the 'BLUEBIRD', and its luxurious interior accommodation. Ample leg room, soft inset lighting, deep concealed luggage containers, smooth running engine — all these features, and many more, make up the finest motor coach ever built. It takes but one journey to convince.

## Alexander's

### ROYAL BLUE MOTOR COACHES

Local Office: ACADEMY STREET, INVERNESS
Telephone 856

Main Booking Office: 473 CATHREDRAL STREET, GLASGOW
Head Offices: BROWN STREET, CAMELON, FALKIRK
and Branches throughout Scotland

*The Bluebird luxury buses, operating between Inverness and the Central Belt cities provided a comfortable and cheaper, if rather slower alternative to the railway in 1935, when this ad appeared in 'Book of the Highlands', a companion volume to 'Book of Inverness', with which it shared many items in common.*

*Staff of Queensgate branch of the Clydesdale Bank gather in the early 1960s at a presentation on their behalf to Helen McIntyre by Hugh Gillespie.*

*Another picture of staff at Queensgate branch of the Clydesdale Bank in the early 1960s – rear, from left: Brian Munro, Neil MacArthur, Edward MacGregor, Sandy Watt; middle, from left: Eleanor MacDonald, Christie Bee, Maureen Bruce, Helen McIntyre, Margaret Mathieson; front, from left: Norman MacKenzie, Hugh Gillespie, George Smith, Helen MacDonald, Sandy Milne.*

**BOOKING OFFICE AND SHOWROOMS:**

## 29 QUEENSGATE

(Opposite Post Office)

**D**AILY PLEASURE TOURS by comfortable and reliable Motor Coaches to Gairloch, lovely Glen-affaric, Lochs and Moorland Tours and Falls of Foyers.

There is no scenery in Scotland to compare with these Tours, each of them with a wealth of grandeur and beauty which cannot be described, or surpassed.

## FRASER AND ELAND
*The Motor Tour Specialists*
## 79 ACADEMY ST.
## INVERNESS

Phone 463          Grams: "Fraser Eland"

*Another advert from the 'Book of the Highlands', circa 1935, a comprehensive guide book to Inverness and the Highlands published in the 1930s, for hirer and tour operator Fraser and Eland, which had its main premises in Academy Street.*

Parcels Service

Season Tickets Available

*Comfortable, Reliable and Punctual Travel . .*

**Between**

**INVERNESS, DINGWALL, STRATHPEFFER, TAIN, DORNOCH, BRORA, HELMSDALE, WICK and THURSO**

**Also between**

**INVERNESS and CROMARTY via KESSOCK or MUIR OF ORD; DINGWALL to CROMARTY**

**Special Tours in ISLE OF SKYE by Motor Coach and Launch**

## 29 BANK STREET, INVERNESS

Telephone No. 371

*An early advert from around 1935 for Highland Transport Co Ltd, formed in 1930 from Inverness and District Motor Services, founded five years before. Over the following six decades it grew and spread throughout the North Highlands, swallowing up many smaller bus operators, being nationalised by the British Transport Commission in 1948, and changing its name once again in 1952 to Highland Omnibuses Ltd, when it took over Macrae & Dick's bus operations. It was run by the nationalised Scottish Bus Group from 1969 to 1991, when in the Government's haste to dispose of almost every state-owned asset, it was sold to the privately-owned Rapson's Group. Some very interesting photographs of Highland's buses appeared in Inverness Remembered IV, contributed by Willie Milne of Ardersier, who has written an excellent illustrated history of the company called simply 'Highland'.*

*A photo of the former Falcon Iron Works, taken in relatively recent times, prior to it being dismantled and rebuilt stone by stone in the new Falcon Square, Inverness.*

**A Ross & Son**                    **Royal Ordnance Lounge, Inverness**

*This interior shot of the long-vanished Royal Ordnance Lounge in Tomnahurich Street, seen here in postcard form, appears to have been taken, judging from the streamers, crown and ER cipher, in the period before the 1953 Coronation.*

This J Arthur Dixon postcard study of the busy Kessock ferryboat 'Eilean Dubh', loved by some and disdained by many, was most likely taken, if the Ford Anglia car awaiting embarkation on the pier is any indication, in the early 1960s, when the Kessock Bridge was still just a fond dream in the minds of a few progressive people. The vessel was referred to by many monoglot English speakers, unaware that her Gaelic name meant Black Isle, as the Eileen Dub! The Kingussie postmark on the back of the card, cancelling the twopence-ha'penny stamp, tantalisingly fails to display the date of posting, but the message on the back, from an undecipherable sender to a Mr G Pettifer of Poole, Dorset, reads: "Having a lovely time soon be home again. Weather not too good today." What's new?

Members of the Scottish Ambulance Service, Inverness, pictured in the early 1970s. They are, rear row, from left: Bob MacAskill, Graham Forbes, Archie MacRae, Evan Gair; middle row, from left: Calum Campbell, Brian Gillingham, Ricky Dallas, Andy Anderson, Kenneth MacKenzie, Keith Fernie, Stewart Walker, Eddie Gillingham; front, from left: Sandy Sutherland, Mrs Miller, Willie Paterson, Roddy Ross, Bob Shand, Norman Garrow, Peter Wemyss.

*Well-known former Inverness baker Thomas Skinner, whose Crown Bakery business on Stephen's Brae survived until the late 20th Century, appears to have just taken delivery of these Ford Model-T vans around 1920, when this photo was taken. It was contributed by Ishbel MacQueen, whose father Alister MacRae, wearing a bonnet, is the largest of the three boys on the right. Mrs MacQueen thinks he may at that time have been a message boy for the firm.*

*The staff of Walker's Sawmills, Inverness, taken in three separate years. The first, taken in 1917, differs greatly in that the majority of employees pictured are women, while most of the males are either young lads or old men outwith the age of military service. There are no women at all in the 1924 picture, their services almost certainly having been dispensed with after the Armistice of 1918, when many of the lads shown here would have returned from the forces. The three ladies in the 1925 photo are probably members of the office staff.*

This photo, taken in January 1955, in the days when Britain still manufactured cars with international cachet, shows Inverness brothers Donald (left) and Hugh Campbell, both mechanics employed by the local Standard Triumph agency, James Ferries & Co Ltd, receiving diplomas from the firm's managing director Marion Jack. They had recently graduated at the manufacturer's Coventry service school as specialists in the repair and maintenance of Standard and Triumph vehicles. They are standing in front of a coveted Triumph TR2 sports car, of which 8,636 were manufactured between 1953 and 1955. On the extreme right is Ferries' foreman Joe Davidson, while behind the car, from left, are George Tyronney, David Bain, Pat MacLeod, John Munro, Alistair MacDonald, Alistair Fraser, Brian Matheson, Bill MacDonald, Billy Moran, Bert Crout, Stan Kennedy and Finlay Campbell. Bill MacDonald, who submitted this photo, was then serving his time as a mechanic with the firm. He recalls that Stan Kennedy was head storeman, and that Pat MacLeod, a shareholder in the company, was a very skilled welder, blacksmith, turner and machinist. Sadly the Campbell brothers, like most of the others in the photo, have since passed on. The TR2, at £956 for the overdrive version, the cheapest car on the market to exceed 100 mph, became a classic, with remaining examples still very much sought after by collectors. There are reckoned to be still around 500 in existence.

Nairn's Photo-Cine Service in Baron Taylor's Street, owned by James Nairn Snr and his sons James Nairn Jnr and Lewis Nairn. From the type of camera on display, this photo appears to have been taken in the early 1950s. The man in the doorway is Ted Hunter.

This picture of William Third, foreman inspector of the Caledonian Canal, based at Clachnaharry, has been passed on to us by his daughter Sheila. From the photograph, he was clearly also a skilled craftsman who approached his responsibilities in a hands-on fashion.

Members of the kitchen staff at Hilton Hospital, Inverness, pictured around 1961. They are rear: C Hendry, June MacDonald, Simon - , Chrissie Robertson, Ella Crawford; front: Marjorie Robertson, Ina - , Margaret Macpherson, Elisabeth Dyce.

*The famous Round House engine shed at Inverness Station, pictured in the 1940s. A symbol of the great days of railway pioneering in the Highlands, it was rudely demolished in the 1960s to make way for "development".*

*The joint retirement ceremony held in 1983 for locomotive drivers Peter Keil and William Lobban. The pair being honoured are standing half-hidden in the back row, fourth and third respectively from the right in the back row, but everyone seems to be very happy.*

British Railways permanent way inspectors pictured at Inverness with the trophy they received collectively for the best district of 1950. They are, rear, from left: Alex MacDonald, Sam Campbell, Malcolm Miurchison, William Fraser, Alex MacDonald, Angus McTavish, Alex Nicolson, John Allison, William Noble; front: Alister Geekie, William Duncan, Robert Mackintosh, Ian Fraser, Alex MacDonald, chief permanent way inspector, John Chisholm, Thomas Campbell.

This photograph was taken in the mid-1950s, just after Inverness-based electrical and mechanical parts wholesalers Thomson & Brown had moved office from Eastgate to new premises at 55-67 Castle Street. Those in the photo are, on left: Unidentified, Elsie Ingram, Pat Mackay, Helen Bruce, George Innes (standing), Chris Innes and Audrey Forsyth.

*This photo was taken in the late 1970s and shows the ex-Inverness Courier staff who defected to Eccles over the previous couple of years. At that time Eccles was the on[ly] lithographic printing firm in town so those interested in the future wanted to get away from the old letterpress system. The line-up here is rear, from left: Bob MacKenzie, Ale[x] MacAskill, Hamish Gordon, Alan Forsyth; front: Donny Ross, John Sinclair, Roddy Tolmie, Billy Robertson. Says Hamish, who contributed the photo: "Ah - them were the days!"*

# BUSINESS AND WORKERS

Older readers may recognise the tall young man on the left of this picture as well-known Inverness journalist the late Jim Love, theatre, jazz and classical music enthusiast, latterly the well-kent and much-respected editor of the 'Inverness Courier', before his death in 2006, aged only 63. At the time of this photo, taken in the Record Rendezvous in Church Street and thought to date from the late 1960s, Jim would have recently moved from the now defunct 'People's Journal' to the 'Press & Journal'. Pictured with him is Anne Munro, a partner in the business with the firm's founder, the late Jack Gordon. Says Jack's son Hamish, who passed on this photo: "The younger generation will probably not recognise the square things in the wall as vinyl LPs!" The offerings on sale here range from albums by Ray Conniff, Tom Jones and Dionne Warwick to Woody Allen, The Supremes and Cliff Richard.

These ladies were employees of a canning factory in operation at Telford Street, near the Caledonian Canal, in the middle of last century. We know that the woman third from the right was called Cathy Kesson, mother-in-law of Kathleen Kesson who submitted the photo, but we haven't been able to identify the others.

# Enterprising agricultural contractor and family

*Inverness millwright William Stewart was quick to perceive the benefits mechanisation could bring to the farming industry, and set up as an agricultural contractor. His grandson James MacKenzie, who contributed this and several other photographs, tells us he acquired the threshing mill in this photograph from Canada, one of the first of its kind in Scotland, and hired it around many farms in the north. It is pictured here with a steam engine, which besides hauling it, also powered it by means of a long belt driven by the huge wheel beside the driving seat. The threshing mill served a wide agricultural community for many decades. James's wife Wilma, who was brought up in Grantown remembers it working on a farm in her area in the late 1950s, though it is likely that its means of power and transport had by that time changed. William Stewart and his wife Isabella lived at Thornton Cottage, Culcabock, where they raised a family of four.*

*This is another photo of William Stewart's threshing mill, being fed with grain from a cart, though the location, like that in the previous picture, is unidentified.*

*This picture, almost certainly taken on the same day as the previous photo, shows bold William Stewart himself on the right, pipe in hand, supervising his machinery.*

*William Stewart and his wife Isabella at the door of their home, Thornton Cottage, Culcabock.*

*The MacKenzie family at 5 Druid Road, Inverness in 1954. They are Margaret, the oldest, her brother William, known as "Wink", sister Pat and baby James, who sent in this photo.*

*Pat MacKenzie with her uncle Dan Grant and cousin Duncan in Inverness High Street in the early 1950s.*

*Three MacKenzie family members pictured in their grandfather William Stewart's garden at Culcabock in 1952 – from left: Margaret, William and Pat.*

*The Stewart family at Thornton Cottage, Culcabock in the inter-war years.*

*Isa Stewart, daughter of William and Isabella, Culcabock, makes use of an old child's cradle as a comfortable resting place for the family dog.*

*Members of William and Isabella Stewart's family pictured outside Thornton Cottage, Culcabock, in the 1920s. They are, from left: Bunty, Will, Dan and Isa. Sadly all have now passed on.*

# Self-made businessman of Imperial era

This photo was taken shortly before the Great War at the mansion in Culduthel Road, Inverness, then known as Kaisarbagh. The trio in the picture, the family of owner James Lyon and his wife Janet, are Isabel, the little girl on the left, with her older siblings Bessie and Louis.

Alan MacLeod, Isabel's son, now living in Edinburgh, tells us the story behind this photo:

"The name Kaisarbagh was given to 41, originally 31, Culduthel Road by my maternal grandfather, James Lyon, a Perthshire man, born at Caputh around 1860. Orphaned at about age eight, he was brought up by his aunt Louise, and became a gunsmith. I know little about his earlier years, but he seems to have worked in Newcastle and London, at one time, possibly, with the famous gunsmiths' firm of Purdey & Purdey. According to the 1881 Census, he was described as a gunsmith and lodging in Inverness with the family of Highland Railway masonry inspector George Batchen, at 6 Innes Street. He subsequently married George's daughter Janet. James then went to Calcutta where he worked for a time for an existing gunsmith, before establishing his own business. A self-made man who spent 40 years, from 1882 to 1922, in India, he was very successful, and travelled all over the sub-continent.

"He bought the Inverness property around 1910, with the intention of retiring, but in the event, he didn't retire until much later, possibly because of the intervention of the Great War. The name he gave the house is Hindi. I understand that it means 'Emperor's or possibly King's Garden.' There is a palace in Lucknow of the same name which figured in the Indian Mutiny. My mother always told me that the name meant 'Lyon's Garden.' I suspect that she (or grandfather) was not strictly correct, but I believe he may have used a little bit of licence and interpreted the Hindi as follows – Emperor's/King's Garden, – therefore Lyon's or King of the Beasts' Garden.

"Having an interest in the use of words, languages, dialects and accents, I find the foregoing extremely interesting and I can understand grandfather's thinking. I am interested that the 'Kaisar' part should have the same meaning as 'Kaiser' in German.

"Incidentally, during the Great War, the name had to be removed from the stone pillars at the front gate as public opinion dictated such action. As so often happens, public opinion misinterpreted the situation, or did not bother to find the facts before taking action. Perhaps the public would have reacted differently if they had realised that my uncle, grandfather's only son, Louis, called after his beloved aunt, was serving with the British Army. He was a civil engineer, and served in both world wars with the Royal Engineers."

Today the mansion that once was Kaisarbagh is still a private residence, although the stone lions on the gate pillars are painted a slightly incongruous silver.

# A landmark factory and its last days

In 1940, as Britain stood alone against the might of Nazi Germany, one small Inverness firm was playing its own vital part in the war effort producing specialist welding equipment. This was the fire pump used at that time by A I Resistance Welders Ltd's staff fire brigade, at the company's Victorian Rose Street Foundry. Fortunately it was never tested in a war situation. The company went on to produce equipment used to manufacture PLUTO, the remarkable pipeline under the ocean, used to pump fuel from Britain to Europe after D-Day. Can any readers identify the firemen?

The lady with the Vauxhall Wyvern of around 1950 vintage, pictured outside her parents' home in now long-demolished Manse Place, Inverness, is Pearl Donaldson, later Wilson. Pearl at that time was secretary to the late James Sinclair, a director of A I Welders Ltd and a leading mastermind behind the construction of PLUTO, the pipeline under the ocean which helped to shorten the war by supplying safely millions of gallons of precious fuel to the Allied forces fighting in Normandy after D-Day in 1944.

Two young colleagues, pictured around 1955, working for the then-flourishing resistance welding machinery manufacturer A I Welders Ltd, which had its headquarters in Academy Street and its extensive factory just around the corner in the Rose Street Foundry. On the left is electrician Jock Kesson, who at time of publication was living in Dalneigh Road, and Uisdean MacCulloch from Ardersier, who later emigrated to Australia.

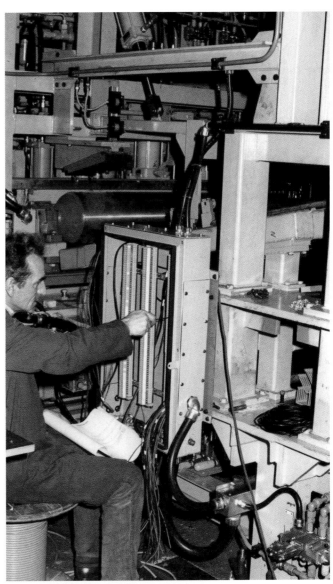

Electrician Jock Kesson working on a complex piece of machinery at his workplace in the former A I Welders Ltd's Rose Street Foundry.

All that remained of the main manufacturing building at Rose Street Foundry on the day it finally closed its doors forever, 6 October 1988, after its owner, A I Welders Ltd, moved to new premises on the Longman Industrial Estate, with a substantially depleted workforce compared to its heyday in the middle of the century. Much of the equipment used to weld PLUTO, the subsea pipeline, was made at Rose Street Foundry.

*A view of the empty Rose Street Foundry on the day it closed its doors for the last time in 1988.*

*The other side of Rose Street with more of A I Welders' premises on the day the firm finally left the town centre. The girl standing in the doorway is Gillian Kesson, whose mother Kathleen took the photo.*

# Pioneer of glass-fibre boats
## – and the sad sequel

In the 1950s, Alexander MacKenzie and his wife Catherine, both qualified hairdressers, were making a good living from their business in Union Street, Inverness, A Robertson & Co, which besides housing a barber's shop, was also a tobacconist's, with a coffee shop in the basement which was something of an exclusive club for professional men from the burgh. Women were only allowed to use it on Saturdays, recalls Alexander's daughter Sandie, who adds: "The place was a fug of smoke, with cigars and cigarettes blazing away."

However, Alexander's real interests lay in yachting and boating. "He was boat-crazy," says Sandie, who lent us the following series of photographs. "There were boats everywhere. In the garage, in the garden, on the river."

So keen on boats was Alexander that in 1955 he set up a small factory called Mouldacraft Products at Thornbush Slipway, where he is thought to have been the first person in Scotland to build small boats from glass-fibre.

Sadly, Alexander MacKenzie's love-affair with boats had tragic consequences. In those days when health and safety legislation was much less rigid, the dangers of working with glass-fibre were little understood, and only five years later, at the age of 47, he died, after a very brief illness, from the effects of inhaling glass fibres, which had apparently pierced his lungs.

*Alexander MacKenzie's tobacconist's and barber's business in Union Street, Inverness, in the early 1950s. The cars we see are a Ford 8 van advertising Grey's cigarettes and a Humber Hawk Mk IV. The same van, showing more clearly the legend "Greys are great", and a picture of a Scots Greys cavalryman in uniform, appears in a similar photograph in Inverness Remembered Volume III.*

*This photo shows the exterior of Alexander MacKenzie's Mouldacraft Products factory at Thornbush in the 1950s.*

*A rare interior photograph of the Mouldacraft Products' factory, showing two men working on a boat, surrounded by a "snowstorm" of white glass fibres, while a woman, possibly Alexander's wife Catherine, looks on. Note that none of the trio is wearing any form of protective clothing or mask, nor would they probably have realised the need for such measures. This method of working sadly led to Alexander's untimely death.*

# MOULDACRAFT PRODUCTS

Pioneers in Scotland with Fibre Glass Small Craft

## Type 10'-6" Yachtsman's Dinghy

Overall length 10' 6". Beam 4' 6". Moulded Depth 2'.

Roomy, stable, and a first-class weight carrier, its light weight makes it an ideal yacht tender. Robust construction and built-in bouyancy tanks makes it safer for the yachtsman and fisherman alike.

Constructed of leakproof moulded fibreglass, these craft are stronger, yet lighter, than wood. Supplied in a permanent two-colour finish, no painting or maintenance of any kind is necessary. Unaffected by climatic changes they can be left out of doors all the year round, and, being considerably lighter than comparable wood craft, they are more easily handled both afloat and ashore.

| | | | | | |
|---|---|---|---|---|---|
| Price Ex-Works | ... | ... | ... | ... | £68 0 0 |
| Oars and Rowlocks (extra) ... | | ... | ... | ... | 4 5 0 |
| Bottom Boards (extra) | ... | ... | ... | ... | 2 15 0 |
| Hull Shell Only (for easy home completion) ... | | | | | 38 0 0 |

Further information on above and other types of moulded fibre glass craft available on receipt of your enquiry direct to

**Mouldacraft Products, 39 Union St., Inverness.**    Phone: Inverness 2224

Or Their Agents

*This was a Mouldacraft Products brochure from the late 1950s. The example illustrated seems a well-designed little vessel, with built-in buoyancy tanks. Are any of the firm's pioneering craft still in use in the area?*

*A finished Mouldacraft dinghy being rowed through its paces on the River Ness.*

*Alexander MacKenzie is pictured here on the River Ness, apparently testing the smallest of his boat types personally for stability, with no sign of any lifejacket.*

*The motor launch Tuffin, not a glass-fibre creation, pictured here at South Kessock, was one of Alexander MacKenzie's other great loves.*

*Alexander's daughter Sandie, right, who contributed this interesting set of photographs, with her brother Peter, front left, and two other unidentified children, pictured around 1957.*

*Sandie MacKenzie pictured in Inverness High Street, circa 1953, with her mother Catherine and granny Annie Gordon.*

*Tragedy was already stalking the happy couple in this sunny wedding photo taken at St Ninian's Chapel, Inverness in April 1966, when Sandie MacKenzie, then aged only 17, married apprentice draughtsman Alan MacNeill, 19, from Barra. They decided to embark on married life in Alan's home island, where he found work, helping his father rebuild the family croft-house, but sadly he died at the age of 23, from kidney failure, leaving Sandie with three infant children. Her oldest daughter Catherine has inherited the family croft in Barra.*

*Four girls at a wedding. Sandie MacKenzie, front, pictured just before her short-lived marriage to Alan MacNeill, with friends, from left, Kathleen Cumming, Cheryl Gordon and Ishbel Cumming.*

*The Cumming family from Inverness, pictured in 1970 at their home in Oban, to which they had moved three years before, on father Gordon's appointment to bank manager there. Gordon's wife Mabel is on the left, with younger daughter Kathleen sitting in front. At the back is elder daughter Ishbel, with her fiancé Reg Taylor, whom she later married. Reg is holding baby Marion MacNeil, whose mother Sandie took the photo, while Marion's sister Catherine is sitting on Gordon's knee. Sadly the little girls' father, Alan MacNeil, had died earlier that year. Four decades on, Marion is information officer for Multiple Sclerosis Scotland. Gordon and Mabel Cumming were formerly enthusiastic members of Inverness Gaelic Choir and feature in pictures of that august organisation elsewhere in this volume. Ishbel and Reg now live in Queensland, Australia.*

# Civic hero who died in the line of duty

It's a salient reminder of life's brevity tha few of today's Inverness citizens have ever heard of Dr John Inglis Nicol, Provost o Inverness from 1840-43, far less realise the influence he had on the welfare of hi adopted burgh.

Indeed his portrait, which once hung ir the Town House alongside those of othe local civic leaders, seems, as this volume goes to print, to have been placed ir storage.

Born at Taewig, near Beauly, in 1788 Nicol was a kinsman of the kenspeckle Provost William Inglis, a merchant and banker who held the office from 1797 1800 and who had entertained Rober Burns at his Kingsmills home in 1787.

Nicol was initially apprenticed to ar Inverness physician called Dr Kennedy before continuing his professiona education in London, where he also served in some leading hospitals. He late studied at the ancient University of Tubingen, in Germany, which conferred on him the degree o MD, before returning to Inverness to set up practice in 1812.

A caring and conscientious doctor, his interests ranged far beyond medicine, and included chemistry, mechanical gadgets and agricultural improvement. He bought a farm at Campfield which included the area now known as Ladies' Walk, and which became the scene of experiment in cultivation and crop testing.

He was responsible for improvements to the flood-prone river embankment, and is also creditec with inventing an early form of power-saw, remarkable in that it not only felled timber with a straigh cut, but could also be used to make bevelled cuts to manufacture staves for barrels used by loca distilleries.

While still young, John Nicol inherited from a relative a failing woollen mill at Holm, on the side of the River Ness. With characteristic vitality he turned the business round, adding new buildings new machinery and superior staff, with the result that it became a source of fine woollen fabric and much-needed local employment. John Nicol was also an enthusiastic proponent of railwa development, though he did not live to see Inverness connected to the south.

His greatest legacy to Inverness, however, was his drive to improve public health and sanitation in a town then often affected by the dreaded disease cholera. In this John Nicol may have had a personal motive, in that a beloved daughter seems to have died in childhood of the same ailment. He worked particularly hard to develop a proper sewage system and to encourage cleanliness, which ne recognised as essential to disease prevention and good health.

Ironically his devotion to his profession led to his own demise. He contracted cholera while attending to infected patients, and died at his home in Murray Place, on 25th September 1849, aged 71.

He and his wife Barbara, who died 12 years later, lie in a corner of the ancient Chapel Street Yard, beneath a relatively modest headstone, which unfortunately has suffered the ravages of time, including a broken column.

We are indebted for the details of Dr Nicol's life to his great-great-great-grand-daughter Helyn Wilson, nee Nicol, a Spanish national who lives in the picturesque village of Mijas, near the resort of Malaga, and is married to Carlisle-born retired businessman Colin Wilson. Helyn, who was

*Helyn Wilson, Provost John Nicol's Spanish great-great-great-grand-daughter.*

educated in England, who lived in Scotland for several years, and who has visited Inverness to research her illustrious ancestor, is unsure of which generation of his family settled in Spain.

*Provost John Nicol's damaged tombstone in Chapel Yard.*

# A musical celebrity and local heroine

Kate Fraser, sadly now almost forgotten, was a celebrated harpist and singer, believed to have been the first woman in the Highlands to have had her voice recorded on the phonograph, or early gramophone.

Indeed her fame as a harpist seems to have reached far beyond the bounds of her home territory, or even Scotland, as she has been described in a contemporary report as an "international harpist".

An able local headmistress, Kate Fraser stamped her musical authority, as well as her educational and organisational skills, quite firmly on the life of Inverness in the late 19th and early 20th Centuries.

The daughter of Glenurquhart weaver Hugh Fraser and his wife Janet, Lewiston, she showed early talent academically and musically, and trained as a "pupil teacher" or apprentice under the supervision of Farraline Park School headmaster, a Mr Finlayson.

She was promoted to mistress at Clachnaharry School, over which she presided successfully for eight years, before moving upward as headmistress of Farraline Park School, where she remained until her death 27 years later at the age of 58. It was, according to her obituary in the Inverness Courier, in June 1918, a post "she held with credit and success".

The obituary stated: "Miss Kate Fraser's gifts as a singer and as a teacher of singing found excellent scope in the school. These gifts and her familiarity with the Gaelic language also made her an enthusiastic supporter of the Mod, for which she was a tireless and greatly appreciated worker for many years. Of the Children's Mod she was practically the founder, as she was also the principal organiser, the success of the junior association lying always near her heart."

Surprisingly perhaps, for one who greatly enjoyed and taught secular music, she was also the Gaelic precentor at the Free North Church, a post surely unusual for a lady to hold at that time in a strict Presbyterian institution.

Shortly after the start of the Great War, Kate Fraser embarked on another mission, as convener of Inverness Citizens' Committee, founded to raise funds to buy treats for servicemen in the trenches and prisoner-of-war camps and to provide entertainment for wounded being treated in local hospitals.

"The value of the services which Miss Kate Fraser rendered personally in and of these objects can hardly be overestimated," said her obituary.

Sadly, as the conflict neared its close, Kate fell ill suddenly with appendicitis, and died of peritonitis and heart failure only 12 days after undergoing an operation at the Royal Northern Infirmary.

She was survived by her 88-year old mother Janet, who was to live for a further seven years, her brother Hugh and a sister.

Kate was buried at Old Kilmore Cemetery, Drumnadrochit. Such was the esteem in which she was held by the military and civil population alike, that when her funeral cortege left a relative's home at Silverwells, Ness Bank, Inverness, it was followed by Inverness-shire's Lord Lieutenant, Colonel Mackintosh of Mackintosh, Bishop Maclean, ex-Provost John Birnie, town chamberlain James Maxwell, Inverness Courier editor and proprietor Evan Barron, senior naval and military officers, soldiers from local regiments, sailors, recovering wounded and nurses, while the streets were lined by crowds including many of her pupils.

Several mourners followed her remains all the way to Kilmore, where a pipe-major of the Cameron Highlanders, dispatched specially from Ireland for the occasion, and a pipe-major of the Seaforth Highlanders, sent from the training base at Cromarty, played Lament for the Children and Lochaber no More at her graveside.

*This mansion, known as Silverwells, where Kate Fraser's last journey began, belonged in the early part of the 20th century to her kinswoman Isabella Batchen, daughter of George Batchen, the former Highland Railway masonry inspector, who died at Slochd, in 1893. Isabella's great-nephew Alan MacLeod, who contributed this photo, says "I suspect that she moved to Ness Bank as a result of her father's death. I presume that Kate Fraser's funeral procession left Silverwells because of the relationship of the Frasers to the Batchens. By 1918, Isabella and her brother, George, the draper and other brothers, Donald, Tom and Alec (when they were at home) would have been resident there.*

*George Batchen (1823-93). was a very able stonemason, who rose up the ranks of his calling to become masonry inspector with the Highland Railway. He died, still working, a* *Slochd, during construction of the direct line from Aviemore to Inverness. He is reputed to have been very much involved with the building of the Tomatin railway viaduct, which his family always referred to as "Batchen's Bridge." George married Elizabeth MacKenzie from Glenurquhart and lived at 6 Innes Street, Inverness, where the couple brought up a a large family. Their daughter Isabella and son George, the draper, thought to be one of the volunteer soldiers in the next picture, later lived at Silverwells, Ness Bank.*

*Two part-time soldiers of 1st Inverness (Highland) Volunteer Battalion of the Cameron Highlanders, pictured in the uniform worn between 1880 and 1893, when the Volunteers were reorganised. Note the quaint muzzle-loading rifles, elderly even by late Victorian standards. Inverness-born Alan Macleod, now living in Edinburgh, believes they are his Batchen great-uncles, Donald, left and George. "I am not sure that the two soldiers depicted in the photo are Batchens, but I believe it to be so. Donald became chief marine engineer of the Blue Funnel Line. George was a draper in Inverness. Another brother, Alexander, was a banker with the British Linen Bank, who went to London, where he lived until his retirement. Another brother, Thomas, was a railway engineer who went to Ireland where he became chief engineer of a railway company."*

# School and college days remembered

*Members of the English and media studies department at Inverness College in the 1980s with head of department, Sandra Macleod, kneeling, left.*

*Students at Inverness College, snapped in the 1980s.*

Inverness Technical High School Class IIA from 1956. The pupils are, rear row, from left: May MacGillivray, Mary MacLeod, Moira Watson, Annie Higgins, Joyce Blackley, Marion Robertson, Annie Watson, Charlene Davidson, Sylvia Ross; second row, from left: Caroline Harrison, Sarah MacDonald, Marjorie McGee, Drina Orr, Irene Smith, Ann Simpson, Pat MacKenzie, Frances Mackie, Marlene McPhillips, Eileen Mellis, Georgina Matheson; third row, from left: Shona Kerr, Christine Sutherland, Ann Scott, Eleanor Tulloch, Marjorie Cuthbert, Miss Lyon (registered teacher), Mamie Hutcheson, Shirley Spence, Elsie Lawless, Norma Larke, Marion Mackenzie; boys, sitting in front, from left: Andrew Goodall, Colin MacLean, Donald Fraser.

Class 3A of Inverness High School, photographed in 1956. Back row, from left: Unidentified, unidentified, unidentified, Cathie Ann Macneil, unidentified, Cathie MacGowan, unidentified, Florrie Carl, Elizabeth Mackenzie. Third row, from left: Jacqueline Kane, Maureen Fleming, unidentified, Sophie Mackenzie, unidentified, Raye Henderson, who submitted this photo, Jean Smith, unidentified, unidentified, unidentified. Second row, from left: - Evelyn Mackenzie, Patricia Chisholm, Elizabeth Yeudall, unidentified, Gilbert Mackenzie, unidentified, unidentified, unidentified, Maureen Balfour, Audrey Banham. Front row, from left: Unidentified, Doreen MacRae, Eileen Mackenzie, Margaret Yeudall, unidentified, Iris Ross, Nancy Macpherson, Sandra Stewart, Morag Dunbar. Eileen Mackenzie, now Mackinnon and living in Skye, and who was able to identify some of those in the photo, says she has a copy with the names signed on the back. She adds: "Names on the back, not given above are: Frances Angus, Catherine Watson, Betty Smart, Moira Roy, Jessie Lee (may be the girl in the middle of the front row, between Margaret and Iris), Jean Fraser (may be the girl at the end of the third row) Ann Watson, Kathleen Forbes (may be girl in third row, third along, next to Maureen Fleming) Eleanor Ross (may be girl on third row, third from right, next to Jean Smith), Charlotte MacGillivray."

*Class 7A at Central Primary School, Inverness, 1953. Rear row, from left: Robert Fraser, David M Henderson, James Carr, Alan Scott, Gilbert Mackenzie, William Paterson, Ronnie -, David L Arthur, Harry Smith, Iain Jack, Iain Rose, Iain MacKintosh. Third row, from left: Miss G M Wilson, Margaret Yeudall, Patricia Chisholm, Valerie Fraser, Joan L Nutney, Annabell Rose, Maureen Balfour, Eileen Milne, Sheila Forsyth, Rosemary Macdougall, Catherine Gordon, Audrey Banham. Second row, from left: Elizabeth Yeudall, Kathleen Taylor, Rena Wallace, Evelyn Mackenzie, Iris Ross, Eileen Mackenzie, Raye D Henderson, unidentified, Morag Dunbar, Christine Ross, Doreen MacRae, Jean MacCallum, Wilma Mackay, Joanna Garrioch. Front row, from left: John Ross, Albert E Mackenzie, Jack Grigor, John Wilson, Robert MacDonald, Campbell Ward. The photo was submitted by Raye Leith, whose classmate Eileen Mackenzie (now Mackinnon), provided most of the names. Eileen, who also has a copy of the photo with names on the back, says: "I have an additional name, Alison Sutherland, but I am not sure if she is the unidentified name in the photo, or whether she was absent when the photo was taken, as her name is in brackets."*

*The late Matt Campbell is remembered by hundreds of former Inverness High School pupils as a well-liked and respected geography teacher, who organised the very popular geography club outings and the annual weekend away hostelling. This picture was taken in 1963 following his promotion to headmaster of Drummond School.*

*Inverness High School pupils at Inverness Station in 1963, at the start of a trip to France and Belgium. The teachers in the middle from left are: Mr Garden, Mr McPhee and Mr McGregor.*

*Inverness High School pupils on trip to Europe, pictured in front of the Atomium in Belgium.*

*This photo of St Joseph's RC School mixed classes choir was taken in front of St Mary's RC Church, after it lifted a trophy at Inverness Music Festival in 1954. Pictured are, rear, from left: John McIntee, Odinea Derman, Tessa Smith, Maybelle Gordon, Rose Ann MacLennan, Jean Lamb, Kathleen Mitchell, Shirley Cameron; middle row, from left: Jimmy Quinn, Sandy Johnston, Frances Tulloch, Mary MacLeod, Mary Fox, Margaret Grimley, Angus Mackay, David Power; front, from left: Hugh MacIver, Tommy MacDonald, Annie Cameron, Mary Cameron, Cathie Gilfeddar, Ada MacIver, Ian Skivington.*

*Pictured here are the tiny tots who made up the large new Primary 1 intake at Hilton Primary School in 1973.*

These smart youngsters were in Primary 7, their final year at Hilton Primary School, Inverness, when pictured in 1979. They are, rear, from left: Mark Walker, David Cooper, Margaret Spence, Gordon MacInnes, Stephen Grant, Colin Mackay; third row, from left: Alison Dyce, Stuart MacLaren, Brian Watson, Neil Moir, Graham Godsman, Graham MacDonald, Catherine Oag, Mrs MacLeod; second row, from left: Allan Wilson, Brian Ferguson, Donna MacDonald, Jackie McArdle, Pamela Gardiner, Colette Longshaw, Tanya MacKenzie, Susan MacKenzie, Steven Gourlay; front, from left: Nicole Ewen, Gordon Grant, Diane Baird, Mary Fitzpatrick, Patricia Mackay, Gary Paul, Jennifer Chisholm and Desmond Harrigan.

Some boarding pupils from Inverness Royal Academy and a master, pictured at Drummond Park Hostel, in the mid-1950s. Their names are given as Rusty, Donald MacLennan, J F Morrison, Mr D Cameron, Lachie MacAulay and Bingo. Where are they now, and can any reader tell us any more about them?

*As contributors' memories fade with the passage of two generations, we only have some names for the children in this Primary 3 photo from Crown Primary School in 1951. They are, rear row, from left: Unidentified, Frances Mackie, Heather Smith, unidentified, Anita Wilson, Patricia -, Jean Campbell, Mabel Sim, Annie Watson, unidentified, unidentified, unidentified, Gavin Currie; middle row, from left: Derek Mackenzie, Alistair Sutherland, Marjorie MacDonald, Christine Sutherland, Eileen Beattie, Rosemary MacGregor, Elma Armstrong, Moira Watson; front, from left: unidentified, Sheila Gunn, unidentified, Sheila Chisholm, Jean Taylor, Marjorie -, Heather Toughie, unidentified.*

*A youthful class at Bishop Eden's School in 1907, now all long passed on, though descendants doubtless still live in the city.*

Pictured here around 1948 are members of Class 5A at Merkinch School. They are, rear, from left: John MacKenzie, Colin MacDonald, John Murphy, A Kaka, Ronald Hughes, James Taylor, Donald Groat, Robert Dewar, James Stewart; third row, from left: James MacKenzie, Cecil Williams, Ernest Chisholm, Bill MacDonald, George Godsman, David Morrison, Alex Fraser, James Elliot, David Shaw, Tommy Miller; second row, from left: Kathleen Dunbar, Lydia Macpherson, Sheila MacKenzie, Isabel Shaw, Catherine Wells, Marion Fraser, Jennifer Morrison, Lily Hendry, Helen MacVicar, Margaret Williamson; front, from left: Peggy Samuels, Joyce Russell, Margaret Lennox, Margaret Wilson, Lillian Mackay, Isobel Stewart, Margaret Johnstone. Their class teacher, not in the picture, was a Miss Steele, from Carbost, in Skye.

Members of Primary 7A at Merkinch School, pictured in 1961. Marjory Dunn, then MacDonald, who sent in this photo, has been able to provide most of the names. Rear row, from left: Bryan Munro, David Thomson, Alec Calder, Ian Junor, Brian Urquhart, Brian Carson, unidentified, Allan Young; third row: John Skinner, Richard (Todd?) Graham Campbell, Hugh Ross, David Miller, John Beattie; second row: Susan Chisholm, Margaret Imlach, Catherine MacLean, Ann Barnett, Evelyn Greer, Marie MacBain, Margaret Allan, Isobel Alexander, Catherine Brown; front row: Marjory MacDonald, Elizabeth MacGillivray, Margaret MacDonald (Marjory's twin), Diane MacAulay, Kathleen Lobban, Sylvia Mackintosh, Evelyn Mackintosh, Ramona MacTavish, Audrey Williamson, Sandra Ross.

*Primaries 3 and 4 of 1950-51 at the long-since defunct Culduthel Primary School.*

*Pupils of Cauldeen School in 1985, with Miss Smart, who seems to be holding a certificate, perhaps a token of her length of service.*

This was the last primary school class to come through Inverness Royal Academy, before the junior school closed in the early 1960s. Sandie Mackenzie, who features in the photo, says: "We were the last primary school class to come through the Academy." She has identified some of her former classmates, including rear, extreme left, Ishbel Cumming, with beside her Alastair Thomson and Susan Fraser, extreme right Roderick MacKenzie. In the middle row are, second from the left, Jean Whittet, whose father was superintendent at Craig Dunain Hospital, and fourth from left Janet Lawson whose father Alan was depute director of education for Inverness-shire. Among those in the bottom row are extreme left, Hazel Raffan, with beside her Sandie, and second from the right Patricia Dow.

Members of Class 2B of 1956-57 at what was then still called Inverness Technical High School. They are rear, from left: Hazel Grace, Elizabeth - , Enya Morrison, Thelma Graham, June Cameron, Lorraine Williams, Jill Fraser, Cathie Cameron, Jeannie Bremner; middle row: Christine Ross, Marjory Tasker, Mary Campbell, Joan Findlay, Sheila Ross, Wilma Chisholm, Irene Scott, Wilma Cameron, Pat Shivas, Marjory Cameron; front row: Ann - , Colena Thomson, Irene Thomson, Coleen Robertson, Janet - , Margaret Urquhart, Catherine Macdonald, Hazel Grace, Jessie Thomson, Mary Urquhart.

By the time this photo was taken the Highland Capital's second senior secondary school had changed its name simply to Inverness High School. The fifth-year class of 1959 - 60 are, rear, from left: Ronnie White, James Macgregor, Christopher Macrae, Derek Mackenzie, Campbell Welsh; second row: Neil Macmillan, Iain Macleod, George Stewart Ian Barron, Douglas Cameron, Watson Munro, David Orrock, James Ferries; third row: depute head, Mr Robertson, Brian Davidson, Annie Watson, Freda Macrae, Irene - Moyra Macgregor, Cathie MacNeil, Caroline Watson, Irene Cameron, Annie Higgins, Donald Fraser; front row: Sylvia Ross, Mary Urquhart, Isobel Little, Sarah Cameron Kathleen Scott, Moira Watson, Marion Robertson, Ronda Miller.

Class 3B of Inverness Royal Academy, pictured in 1956, near the end of session - rear, from left: Robert Lindsay, Ian Fraser, Peter Willis, Roderick Mackintosh, Lennox Latham third row: James Livingstone, Lawrence Harris, Gordon MacDonald, Alexander J MacDonald, Alexander H MacDonald, Iain MacLennan, Donald Cameron, John Urquhart David MacCallum, William Ledingham; second row: Isla MacFadyen, Wendy Cooper, Patricia MacDonald, Marion Gillies, Daphne Robertson, Marilyn Woodward, Suzann McAfee, Julia Urquhart; front row: Catherine Moran, Rosalind MacLeod, Joan MacDonald, Janet Roy, Mrs MacDonald, Alexandra MacDonald, Sheena MacLean, Catherin Grant, Janet Campbell.

*Mrs Fraser's Primary 3 class at Central Primary School, 1966. The children are, rear, from left: Gordon MacDougall, Michael Watt, John Gordon, Ewen Munro, Neil Fraser; third row: Raymond Murray, Neil Johnstone, George MacLennan, Hugh Fraser, Michael Hutchison; second row: Angela Sutherland, Alison Mackenzie, Anne Calder, Carol Grant, Eileen Turnbull, Moira Sanderson, Catherine Suttie, Suzanne Urquhart; front: Cathie Campbell, Marion Peters, Sandra Nott, Gwendoline Munn, Barbara Swanson, Neilian Campbell, Jennifer Sutherland.*

*There's something very poignant for the elderly fond parent about looking wistfully at the photo of a Primary 1 class over 40 years on, with the children now in early middle age and in many cases parents or even grandparents themselves. Pictured here are the "wee ones" of session 1968-69 from Crown Primary School. What has become of them?*

*Another happy Primary 1 class photo from Crown Primary School, this time from session 1970-71.*

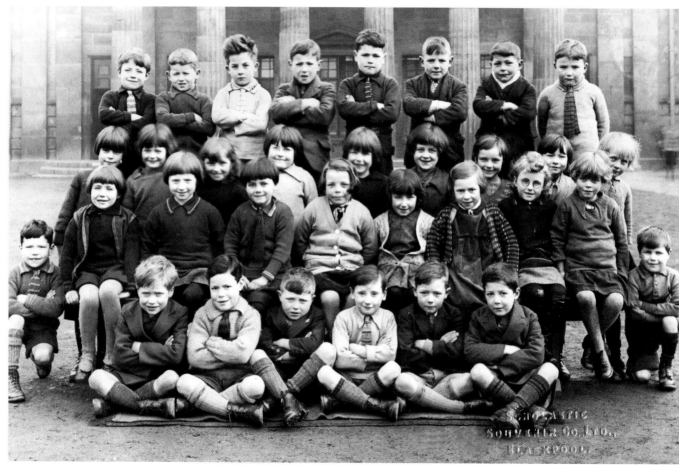

*Pupils of Bell's School, Farraline Park, pictured around 1930. The building, opened in 1841 and now the city library, ceased to be a school in 1937.*

# Celebration and relaxation

Inverness solicitor Jeff Macleod, rear, with his late wife Sandra, right, their son Ian and Sandra's cousin Nan Macdougall, who then owned a soap-making workshop in a former church at Kirkhill, pictured at a family wedding over 40 years ago.

Jeff Macleod, centre, enjoying a New Year's Day dram over 30 years ago with his son Ian and late neighbour Willie Mackay, a handyman who lived for much of his life at Pier Cottage, Aldourie, but came originally from Durness, Sutherland. Ian, who now lives in Edinburgh, is in charge of mapping for the Forestry Commission.

*The wedding, at Drummondhill House, Inverness, in September 1930, of local GP Dr Ian Macleod and Frances Sime. Others in the photo are from left: Ian's father Professor the Rev John Macleod, former minister of the Free North Church, Inverness, and at that time principal of the Free Church College, Edinburgh, his wife Margaret, Inverness solicitor Duncan MacNeil, local businessman, father of the bride and owner of Drummondhill Frank Sime, and bridesmaid Dr Isabel Macleod, also a GP. When the National Health Service came into operation in 1948, Ian Macleod's practice, still in operation and known as the Riverside Practice, was the largest in Inverness.*

*A very young Jeff Macleod in his posh pedal car, watched by his mother Frances (left, partially-hidden) and aunt Elsie Lyon.*

*Cummings Hotel in Church Street was the venue in late 1968 for this triple 21st birthday party, held by the three young men in the middle of the second row from the front. The trio, from left are Douglas Scott, Chalmers Proudfoot and John Matheson. The picture was submitted by Chalmers, a retired quarry manager, now living at Gairloch. Sadly Douglas died tragically in a climbing accident less than two years later. John, a retired police officer, lives at Munlochy.*

*Pat Tait and Bunty Reid, as they were when this photo was taken, were originally from the Ferry area. Now both sadly departed, they remained bosom friends all their lives. Bunty's son Philip Owen, who submitted the picture, thinks it was taken in the late 1940s. He tells us his mother, who was born in 1926 and died in 2003, was at that time working in the former NAAFI bakery in Diriebught Road, and he believes that Pat may have worked alongside her. Pat's married name was Manson. A photo of Philip's father George Owen, a driver with Burnett's Bakeries, appeared in an earlier issue of Inverness Remembered.*

*This photo was taken during the annual pilgrimage to Craig Phadrig summit by members of Masonic Lodge St Columba 1295 in the 1940s.*

*West Church Girl Guides in 1955-56.*

A sea of very happy faces at the Bakers' Union children's Christmas party held in Burnett's Tea Rooms, Academy Street, in 1951. "These were fantastic parties, keenly anticipated and greatly enjoyed," said Joyce MacKenzie, nee Blackley, who is in the photo. "We were each given a gift worth £2 or £3, which was a lot of money in those days, while the Bakers' Union also organised bus trips for members' children." She also recalled that the union also held dances every Saturday night at St Mary's Hall, to raise money for these events.

Children from Telford Gardens at the Coronation Day party in St Mary's Hall, Huntly Street, June 1953.

*Adults from Telford Gardens at the Coronation Day party in St Mary's Hall, Huntly Street, June 1953.*

*Ladies Night for Lodge St Columba 1295, some time in the 1940s.*

*A night out in the Masonic Club in 1981 in honour of keen Freemason Joe Blackley (centre with glasses) and his wife Anne.*

*The golden wedding celebration of well-known and long-serving Inverness milkman James Donaldson and his wife Margaret, pictured here with members of their family and friends at the Tower Hotel, in the late 1950s.*

*The "princess", the little girl on the extreme right, in this delightful photo taken outside Central School nearly 60 years ago, was Raye Henderson, now Raye Leith, who submitted it, while the "king" was classmate David Henderson, no relation. The occasion was a pageant depicting the fable about the king who ordained that his beautiful daughter should only marry a man who could tell him an endless tale, on pain of beheading if he failed. Many suitors failed in their attempts, until one began a story of locusts stealing corn from a vast barn. It repeatedly went "And another locust came and carried away another grain of corn" for so long that the king grew weary and let the man marry his daughter. Maureen Fleming, now Lawson and living in Australia, the little girl on the right of the back row, says: "The rest of us mere mortals were serfs or locusts – the females were the locusts!" Others in the photo are thought to be, rear from left: Peter Sharp, Margaret Mackay, unidentified, Edwin Fox, Iris Ross; front, from left: Iain Jack, John Wilson, Albert Mackenzie, unidentified, Lloyd Arthur, George Black. See some pupils' names signed on the back in the next photo. The boys' uniforms seem just a little incongruous, especially David's which resembles closely that of the pre-war Italian Balilla or Slavic Sokol fascist youth groups.*

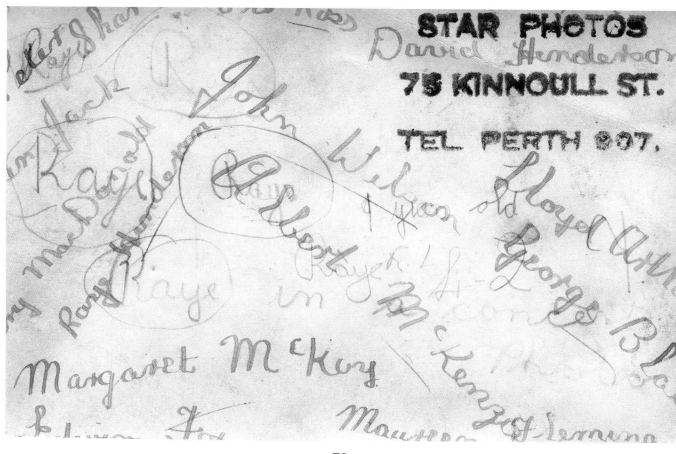

A "bride and two little bridesmaids" make last-minute adjustments to their attire, prior to taking part in a mannequin parade held by fashionable Union Street drapers Young and Chapman, at the Caledonian Hotel ballroom in April 1947, in aid of funds for the National Association of Boys' Clubs. The tiny girl on the left is Raye Henderson, now Raye Leith, who passed this on to us. She can't remember the names of the other two, but recalls: "I was a bit scared, because I was standing on a glass-topped table. At the end of the night I was given a soft, fluffy duck for my part." Among the helpers was well-known North of Scotland sprinter Ian C Young.

This quintet of revellers was snapped at sunrise on the summit of Craig Phadrig on May Day 1972. The bearded chap on the extreme left is Graeme Souter, then a teacher at Millburn Academy, while the lass in the middle, who lent us the photo, is Elaine Gray, then teaching at Beauly and now, as Elaine Spowart, retired and married in Northumbria. Can any reader name the others?

*Local rock stars Alastair MacBean "Beans" (right) and Drew Ross of the group Sunshine wow the crowds at a hall fund-raising fete held by Lochardil Scouts at Macdonald Park in June 1981. The boys in the foreground holding balloons are Frazer Gillespie (left) and David Hunter (right), while between them is Ian Cameron.*

*Alistair MacBean (left) and Drew Ross of local pop group Sunshine pick the winning raffle tickets at a hall fund-raising fete held by Lochardil Scouts at Macdonald Park in June 1981, watched by Gordon Gillespie of the 21st Lochardil Scout Group council.*

The Provost of Inverness takes the salute at a military parade along High Street around half a century ago. Can any reader identify the occasion? The marchers are all wearing para smocks, and the soldiers at the rear of the column are wearing the badge of the Parachute Regiment, while the man in front may be wearing a Royal Marines badge. The picture was taken before a fire which destroyed the original F W Woolworth's store. The Provost in the photo is thought to be Allan Ross, who held the office from 1961-1964.

These youngsters were pictured at the Playhouse Cinema in 1953, receiving prizes for a colouring-in competition from the junior Canadian stars of the newly-released film The Kidnappers Jon Whitely and Vincent Winter, who signed the prizes. The adults are left, Mr Macdonald, the projectionist, and cinema manager Jimmy Nairn. The little girl standing at the front, left, is Margaret Cameron, and beside her is Alan Chisholm, while the wee lass with the ribbon, front, left, is Sylvia MacLennan. Can any reader identify the others?

Forty years ago, in November 1971, when the Tories still enjoyed a considerable presence North of the Border, not to mention many attractive young supporters, "Lovely Lass of Inverness" Fiona Fraser was chosen as Miss Scottish Young Conservatives, and who, apart from her rivals for the title, could possibly disagree? This picture was taken later in her year-long reign, in what seems from the budding tree behind to be spring, in the Ness Islands. Fiona, now Mrs Dishington and living in Nairn, is still an active businesswoman in her home city, where for many years she has owned a children's wear shop.

Another photo of Miss Scottish Young Conservatives 1971-72 pin-up girl Fiona Fraser, snapped in Inverness with well suntanned, if not so lovely Prime Minister Edward Heath, while behind her is the then Scottish Secretary Gordon Campbell, later ennobled as Lord Campbell of Croy.

Tommy Cameron was a photographer and public relations man, but continued a weekend sideline as musician and comic. Here, at a wedding, he performs his favourite party piece, "Jock the Peg", a variation on the character created by Rolf Harris.

Duncan Macintyre and Isabella Fraser, both from Portree, Skye were married at Inverness in December 1913. This photo was taken at the back of the former Caledonian Hotel, demolished to make way for a modern excrescence in the mid-1960s.. The couple later founded the Portree newsagents Fraser Macintyre which is still run by descendants of the family. Jamie Angus, who contributed this picture says: "Isabella's cousin Donald Fraser was my great-grandfather. He can be seen in the top row of the photo, second from the left. His brother Harry is on the far right of the same row and sister Lizzie is the lady seated at the left end of the front row. At that time they all lived at 1 High Street, Clachnaharry. I am sure that there will be other Inverness faces in the photo as well. Isabella's brother Donnie is at the far right of the second row, He was headmaster of Braes School in Portree and during World War I was among the youngest in the British army to reach the rank of major at age 26. The photo was sent me by Kate Cumming in Oban who is a descendant of Duncan and Isabella. He was probably best remembered by some as the best shinty player who ever came out of Skye. Donnie known as the 'Wee Major', died tragically in September 1931 at the age of only 41, and was buried in the new cemetery at Portree. Sadly, most of his siblings never reached the age of 50. His sister Isabella, the bride, also died in her 40s. The lady to the right of the bride in the photo is another sister Mima, who ran a boarding house in Portree with her husband Willie Ross. I believe it was located on the floor above Fraser Macintyre."

Painter Donald Fraser married Annie Dallas in 1916, in the middle of the Great War, in which he served. The couple subsequently spent most of their adult life in Bruce Gardens, Dalneigh. They celebrated their Golden Wedding anniversary there in 1976, the year before Donald's death. They're seen here being congratulated on the occasion by Provost Ian Fraser.

Some Highland Regional Council employees pictured at a Christmas get-together in 1990. In the photo are, rear, from left: Peter Bales, Gary Warburton, Craig Lawrence, Pete Malin, Jamie Macpherson, Barry Wilson, Brian Lovett; third row, from left: Maryeliana Cameron, Sandra MacLean, Rozlyn MacDonald, Linda Lamb, Andrea Blake, Marjor Walker, Pauline Stevenson, Caroline Johnstone, Megan Macintyre; second row, from left: Carol Beaton, Gillian -, Sheena MacRae, Fiona Urquhart, Emmy MacLean, Haze Forsyth, Diane -, Helen Thomson; front, from left: Ruby Billet, Angela O'Neil, Audrey Mackay, Kieran -, Jennifer -.

*Scottish Ambulance Service members from Inverness in party mood, one Christmas in the early 1970s. Rear, from left: Willie Keegan, Roddy Ross, Des Passmore, Mrs Grant, Alastair Gair, Stewart Walker, Willie Leslie; front, from left: William Hunter, Alistair Ferguson, Ally Newlands, Bob Shand, Evan Gair.*

*Congregation members pictured at Dalneigh Church's millennium party in 2000.*

*A staff dance of Scottish Agricultural Industries, held in the old Caledonian Hotel. Contributor Alan MacLeod is fourth from the right in the back row, beside his late wife Gwen.*

*Away back in the 1950s and 1960s John Wilson's Inverness-based dance band was very popular at country dances in the burgh and outwith on Friday and Saturday nights. Sadly John, left, the quintet's leader and accordionist, died in January 2010, leaving the youthful-looking drummer, Billy Nelson, its only survivor. The other three members, from left, are George Ross, bass; Jimmy Wilson, fiddle and Flora Macpherson, piano.*

Sadly most of the happy band in this formal dinner photo from around half a century ago have since passed on. The couples are, from left: James S Nairn, the well-known former Playhouse Cinema manager and his wife Mary, local plasterer Mr Johnstone and his wife, Mr and Mrs MacDougall of MacDougall's Hotel, Mr and Mrs Cullins, Alasdair MacDougall and his wife Marie, Lewis Nairn and his wife Sheila, James Nairn Jnr and his wife Jane.

A sample of Jimmy Nairn Snr's artistry from the Playhouse Cinema café of over 40 years ago, showing his grandchildren inside a fairyland coach, from left: Alan Nairn, Fionn Nairn, Jennifer Nairn, Peter Nairn, Calum Nairn and Stewart Nairn. This photo was submitted by Sheila Simmons, wife the late Lewis Nairn. Jimmy often enlisted the help of his sons James Jnr and Lewis to help with his artistic creations.

Many of the Highland Capital's great and good were present at the wedding at St Ninian's RC Chapel of Billy Milson and Linda Bernardi on 1st July 1972. Linda's father Mario Bernardi, who had a shop in Stephen's Brae, was also at that time a senior bailie in Inverness Town Council. This explains the presence of several prominent council members and officials, including the late former Provost William "Bobo" Mackay, far right, burgh chamberlain Derek Bigg beside him, the late Provost William Smith, incumbent of that ancient office at the time, third from right, Bill Fraser, later to be provost of Inverness District Council, fourth from left and the late Duncan Chisholm, kiltmaker, far left. Mario himself is peeping out from behind, ninth from left. Now approaching their ruby anniversary, the couple live at Bletchley, near Milton Keynes, while Billy still runs a family exterior decorating business in London, helped by their two sons, Andrew and Ian. Linda recently retired after 40 years' teaching service. Best man, Billy's twin brother Keith, still lives in Inverness.

Here, from contributor Wilma MacKenzie, we show a scene from the old Caledonian Hotel, with the date on the back of the photo given as 13 January 1939. Coincidentally, we learn from a similar photo from contributor Raye Leith that the occasion was Clachnacuddin Football Club's fancy dress ball. We also know that the natty chap in evening suit and bow-tie, judging the costumes, was Landon Sorrel, actor-producer of the Little Theatre, a facility for amateur actors based at the former YMCA Hall in Ardconnel Street. Among happy prizewinners noted in Raye's photo were Cecil Fraser, John Henderson, Molly Donaldson, Tenby Fotheringham and D Campbell. John and Molly later married and became Raye's parents. Landon Sorrel took over management of the Little Theatre in August 1938, shortly after his predecessor, Ronald Macdonald Douglas, left in a fit of pique, having claimed "he had been execrated by the people he employed". Does anyone know any more about these two colourful characters?

*Inverness Gaelic Choir's male voice section, pictured with their trophy in the early 1960s.*

*Inverness Gaelic Choir pictured in the early 1960s. Does anyone know the year or the venue?*

A note on the back of this photograph tells us that the lady sheltering behind the windbreak was May MacGillivray, and that it was taken by a Miss Gregor "on the Golf Course" June 1935, at a fete held by Inverness Royal Infirmary, though it doesn't specify which of the burgh's golf courses it was.

Hospital Board staff members at Reay House, Inverness, enjoy a wee celebration around 1960 with rather more than the "light refreshments" one might have expected from such an organisation at that time. It's interesting to note that the three nearest the camera are all smoking – an activity on National Health Service premises which in the 21st Century would merit at least strict disciplinary action, if not instant dismissal. The man second from the left is board driver Angus MacKenzie, whose son James lent us this photo.

Staff of the now sadly long-defunct Burnett's Bakery enjoying themselves at their Christmas dance in the early 1970s.

Another picture from the early 1970s of Burnett's Bakery staff enjoying themselves at Christmas.

A reunion of former Culduthel Hospital staff in 1990.

Perhaps 10-year old Jayne Ahearn was a wee bit nervous about having her photo taken with the inter-company trophy her unit of the Girls' Brigade, B (Cauldeen) Company, attached to Ness Bank Church, had won in 1981. Each member of the winning team was allowed to keep it for a short while.

Many readers of a certain age will remember the open-air concerts and dances held in the Ness Islands during the summer for the benefit of tourists and locals alike. Here is such a scene, with a band playing in the pavilion, which fell into decay and was eventually demolished in the 1980s.

Young and old appeared to be enjoying themselves when this picture of Coronation celebrations was taken at North Kessock in 1953.

We don't know a great deal about who the folk pictured here are, or where the venue was, except that the photo was taken at the staff dance of the grocery chain Cooper's Inverness branch in the early 1930s.

Fun and frolics at the Caledonian Hotel, when the staff of Arnott's department store held their annual dinner dance in 1973.

*Castle Snack Bar staff and friends enjoying an evening out at the Drumossie Hotel around 1970.*

*Don't be fooled by the tinsel streamers in this photo, which give the impression of a Christmas celebration. The folk here are National Union of Public Employees' Highland Area health service branch executive and Scottish executive members, pictured at a branch dance in August 1974. It was submitted by former NUPE Highland branch secretary Brian Corbett, a retired psychiatric nurse, seen here third from right in the back row.*

# The way it was – within living memory

This politically-charged photo of Highland Liberal luminaries was taken, according to information on the back of the original, on 11th August 1973, six months before the first of two general elections to be held the following year. Although the location isn't stated, it was probably at the Inverness home of the man in the middle, holding the baby, none other than celebrated local MP the late Russell Johnston, dressed uncharacteristically in trousers and sweater, rather than his trademark kilt. Others in the picture are, from left, local party publicity officer Bill Mackenzie, Tom Stewart, Arthur Pollitt, Mike Burnett, Dornoch, solicitor Jeff Macleod, and John Robertson, Nigg, prospective parliamentary candidate for Ross and Cromarty. John came third, behind sitting Conservative Hamish Gray and controversial SNP candidate Willie Macrae, with 4,621 votes, but did not contest the October election. Invernessian Hamish, who like Russell, ended his political career in the House of Lords, polled 7,908 votes on the first occasion, but although he increased this to 7,954 a few months later, came near to defeat by Willie Macrae, who in October increased his vote to 7,291.

*A view of the Castle in the late 1950s, taken shortly before the spectacular old suspension bridge was demolished. The shops nearest the river in Bridge Street and Castle Tolmie had already demolished, to make way for the construction, a few years later, of the appalling public library cum offices complex which still blights the riverside vista.*

*The shape of further atrocities to come - like alien modules from a science-fiction scene the Three Disgraces forming the Bridge Street development disfigure the riverside scene in this 1960s photo. Picturesque Queen Mary's House, on the corner of Bridge Street and Bank Street, still stands, but not for much longer, as do some neighbouring buildings, including the 18th Century Caledonian Hotel and Provost Ross's House, which like it were demolished to make way for further "progress" in the shape of a second headquarters building for the burgeoning Highlands and Islands Development Board quango, a concrete replacement hotel akin to a block of contemporary council flats and some even more dreary public service buildings. Thankfully the former Inverness Courier building survives to this day, thanks to eccentric, opinionated but popular editor and proprietor Eveline Barron OBE MA – she loved her post-nominal letters – who resisted all developers' blandishments to sell out.*

*This photo of a large concourse on the Ness Bridge can be dated fairly accurately to the late 1960s, as the excrescences known as the Bridge Street Development already disfigure the skyline on the right, but Queen Mary's House still stands on the corner of Bridge Street and Bank Street, as do some neighbouring buildings also demolished around 1970 to make way for developers' profits and increased rateable values. If memory serves us correctly, the replacement building for Queen Mary's House was financed largely by the Norwich Union insurance company, which at that time boasted as its logo a stylised image of its home town's skyline, together with the motto: "A Fine City Norwich." Clearly the aesthetics of the Highland Capital's new skyline didn't figure prominently in the company's business plan.*

*Union Street in the 1950s, when Britain was still a prominent manufacturing nation, depending for its wealth nearly as much on such heavy industries as motor production as on the leprechaun gold of today's shaky financial system. Only one car visible, the third from the right, a 1938 American Chrysler, is of foreign design. The others include an Austin Cambridge, left, a Morris Oxford from the early part of the decade, second from right, a Jaguar Mk VII, a little white Austin A30 and farthest away a later Morris Oxford. Thankfully this particular view, from the front of the long-demolished Caledonian Hotel, has not changed too drastically over the past 60 years. Melven Brothers' bookshop then still bore its long-established name, although the last of the family in charge had died a soldier's death in the Western Desert campaign of World War II.*

*The former Suspension Bridge, showing behind, the pillar of the "temporary" bridge which alleviated the traffic situation for over 20 years, until the new bridge was opened in 1961. The car crossing appears to be an early Standard Vanguard of the late 1940s or early 1950s.*

*British cars still predominated when this picture of Academy Street was taken in the 1960s, long before Macrae & Dick, right, moved its premises to the Longman Industrial Estate.*

*Another 1960s photograph, this time of Castle Street, while part of the Town House ground floor was still occupied by shops. The "C" registration on the tiny motor cycle indicates that it dates from 1965 or shortly thereafter.*

*Castle Street car park in the 1960s. Note the Bentley limousine in front of MacMillan's Stores. Among the interesting British motor makes now departed are Austin A35s, Ford 100 Populars, Vauxhalls, a Standard 10, a Triumph, an Austin Cambridge, a Hillman Husky and a Hillman Minx. The large car making its way towards the bottom of Castle Street looks like a British Motor Corporation product, possibly a Wolseley.*

*Even during the extremely cold winter of 1947, little boys wore short trousers, as demonstrated here by Tommy Cameron, left, and his wee brother Allan, at their home at 10 Lindsay Avenue.*

**ROYAL BURGH OF INVERNESS**

# DECLARATION

OF

# VICTORY IN EUROPE

## NATIONAL DAY
## :: OF PRAYER ::

On SUNDAY, 13th MAY 1945

## OFFICIAL SERVICE

IN

## OLD HIGH CHURCH, INVERNESS

At 3 p.m.

**The Rev. James Wright, M.A., presiding**

Robert Carruthers & Sons, Printers, Inverness

*The Royal Burgh of Inverness held an official service of thanksgiving at the Old High Church on Sunday, 13 May 1945, five days after the declaration of Victory in Europe. The following pictures show the order of service. The proceedings, while greatly welcome, were no doubt slightly muted by the fact that many local service personnel were still involved in bitter fighting in Burma, or with the Pacific Fleet, and would continue to do so for a further three months, until 15 August, when Japan surrendered unconditionally.*

# Order of Service

## NATIONAL ANTHEM

PSALM 100 .............................................. Tune—"OLD HUNDREDTH"

1. All people that on earth do dwell,
   Sing to the Lord with cheerful voice,
   Him serve with mirth, his praise forth tell,
   Come ye before him and rejoice.

2. Know that the Lord is God indeed;
   Without our aid he did us make;
   We are his flock, he doth us feed,
   And for his sheep he doth us take.

3. O enter then his gates with praise,
   Approach with joy his courts unto :
   Praise, laud, and bless his name always,
   For it is seemly so to do.

4. For why ? the Lord our God is good,
   His mercy is for ever sure;
   His truth at all times firmly stood,
   And shall from age to age endure.

### CALL TO PRAYER — PRAYER
REV. JOHN R. REID

PSALM 124 (Second Version) .............................................. Tune—"OLD 124TH"

1. Now Israel
   may say, and that truly,
   If that the Lord
   had not our cause maintain'd;

2. If that the Lord
   had not our right sustain'd,
   When cruel men
   against us furiously
   Rose up in wrath,
   to make of us their prey;

3. Then certainly
   thry had devour'd us all,
   And swallow'd quick,
   for ought that we could deem;
   Such was their rage,
   as we might well esteem.

4. And as fierce floods
   before them all things drown,
   So had they brought
   our soul to death quite down.

5. The raging streams,
   with their proud swelling waves,
   Had then our soul
   o'erwhelmed in the deep.

6. But bless'd be God,
   who doth us safely keep,
   And hath not giv'n
   us for a living prey
   Unto their teeth,
   and bloody cruelty.

7. Ev'n as a bird
   out of the fowler's snare
   Escapes away,
   so is our soul set free :
   Broke are their nets,
   and thus escaped we.

8. Therefore our help
   is in the Lord's great name,
   Who heav'n and earth
   by his great pow'r did frame.

### OLD TESTAMENT LESSON—ISAIAH XXVI., 1-13
Provost HUGH MACKENZIE, C.B.E., J.P.

### TE DEUM

### NEW TESTAMENT LESSON—ST MATTHEW VII., 15-29
Major-General A. L. COLLIER, C.B.E., M.C.

### PRAYER OF INTERCESSION AND COMMEMORATION
Rev. D. LYNDESAY SMITH, M.A., R.A.F.

HYMN 220 .............................................. "For All the Saints"

1. For all the saints who from their labours rest,
   Who Thee by faith before the world confessed,
   Thy Name, O Jesus, be for ever blest.
   Hallelujah !

2. Thou wast their Rock, their Fortress, and their Might;
   Thou, Lord, their Captain in the well-fought fight;
   Thou, in the darkness drear, their one true Light.
   Hallelujah !

3. O may Thy soldiers, faithful, true, and bold,
   Fight as the saints who nobly fought of old,
   And win, with them, the victor's crown of gold.
   Hallelujah !

4. O blest communion, fellowship divine !
   We feebly struggle, they in glory shine;
   Yet all are one in Thee, for all are Thine.
   Hallelujah !

5. And when the strife is fierce, the warfare long,
   Steals on the ear the distant triumph song,
   And hearts are brave again, and arms are strong.
   Hallelujah !

6. The golden evening brightens in the west;
   Soon, soon to faithful warriors cometh rest;
   Sweet is the calm of Paradise the blest.
   Hallelujah !

7. But, lo ! there breaks a yet more glorious day;
   The saints triumphant rise in bright array;
   The King of Glory passes on His way.
   Hallelujah !

8. From earth's wide bounds, from ocean's farthest coast,
   Through gates of pearl streams in the countless host,
   Singing to Father, Son, and Holy Ghost,
   Hallelujah !

### ADDRESS :—Lt.-Col. T. N. FRASER, M.A., D.A.C.G.

### OFFERING FOR THE CHRISTIAN RECONSTRUCTION OF EUROPE

### PRAYER OF DEDICATION

PARAPHRASE 18 (Verses 3-7) .............................................. Tune—"Glasgow"

The beam that shines from Sion hill
shall lighten ev'ry land;
The King who reigns in Salem's tow'rs
shall all the world command.

Among the nations he shall judge;
his judgments truth shall guide;
His sceptre shall protect the just,
and quell the sinner's pride.

No strife shall rage, nor hostile feuds
disturb those peaceful years;
To ploughshares men shall beat their swords,
to pruning hooks their spears.

No longer hosts encount'ring hosts
shall crowds of slain deplore :
They hang the trumpet in the hall,
and study war no more.

Come then, O house of Jacob ! come
to worship at his shrine;
And, walking in the light of God,
with holy beauties shine.

### "GOD SAVE THE KING"

### BENEDICTION

It's the late summer of 1960, as work is progressing quickly on the new Ness Bridge, and just after the first span has been laid in place, secretary Sandra Fraser, at that time working for consulting engineers Murdoch MacDonald, becomes the first person to make this rather perilous crossing, along with the late Willie Logan, boss of Muir of Ord-based Duncan Logan Ltd, the contractors. Only six years later the genial tycoon, who had been involved in the construction of many hydro-electric schemes, roads and bridges, and who founded the air service Loganair in 1962, died when his private aircraft crashed in mist on Craig Dunain, a few miles from the city centre. It's doubtful if Sandra, now Wilson, and retired, would be permitted by health and safety regulations to undertake such a hazardous trip.

A gathering of Sunday school teachers at Inverness Methodist Church, around 1955. They are, rear, from left: Gary Shaw, Rita Ledingham, Kitty Cameron, Isobel Henderson, Margaret Mackenzie, Ena Cameron, unidentified, Morag Burns, Phyllis Philips, Ruth Pryor, Betty Mackintosh, unidentified; front row, from left: Mr Campbell, unidentified, Mr Thomson, Rev J R Reid, Mrs Reid, Mrs Lindsay, unidentified, unidentified; kneeling in front, from left: Ellen Richmond, Sandra Fraser.

*A gathering of Inverness Young Homemakers at the Cummings Hotel, around 1976.*

*This splendid study of the River Ness from Bank Street by versatile cinema manager, cine-photographer and still photographer Jimmy Nairn, dates from around the early 1950s. The picturesque Suspension Bridge, demolished in 1960, and handsome Castle Tolmie, recalled by hundreds of Invernessians as the building housing a dentist's surgery, are still intact.*

These lads were members of 6th Inverness Company, Boys' Brigade, from St Mark's Church, pictured around 1952. They are, rear, from left: John Miller, Billy Robertson, Charlie Gunn, - Hobban, Billy Nelson, unidentified, - Tulloch, unidentified, unidentified, David MacIver; centre, from left: John Godsman, unidentified, - Robertson, unidentified, A MacOwan, David Shaw, Simon MacKenzie, David Rooney; front, from left: Bill MacDonald, David Morrison, Sonny Sutherland, Jackie Ross, Captain Willie Hossack, Rev John Graham, Hamish Mackintosh, Frank Finlayson, Henry Nelson. Hamish Mackintosh later became captain of the 11th Company BB when it was formed.

A later photo of 6th Inverness Company Boys' Brigade members who took part in a fund-raising variety concert around 1956 in the Little Theatre, Farraline Park, now the City Library. In the photo are, rear, from left: Dave Paterson, John Miller, Rev John Graham, Ronnie MacKenzie, Bill MacDonald, Billy Milton, David Hardie, Henry Nelson, Captain Willie Godsman, Stanley Bryan; centre, from left: James Sheerin, Harry Douglas, George MacDonald, Ronald Collie, Frank Finlayson, James Severn, Robert Severn, Robert Wilson; front, from left: Tommy Reilly, Bruce Gibb, Derek MacRae, Stanley MacMillan, Ian Barron, Tommy Rooney, Willie Rooney, Alistair MacLennan.

*The inimitable Jimmy Nairn himself, with two historic posters from his large collection, snapped probably in the 1970s. Jimmy, who managed the Playhouse Cinema for over 30 years, until its untimely demise by fire in 1972, spent many hours in the later part of each year decorating the buildings foyer and restaurant with Disneyland themes, to the delight of visiting children – and their parents.*

*An early postwar photo taken somewhere out in the countryside surrounding Inverness, showing Jimmy Nairn Snr and his younger son Lewis beside a handsome Humber saloon dating from the mid-1930s.*

*A study of Inverness Castle from the Raining's Stairs, taken in 1962.*

*The "temporary" Ness Bridge, which for over 20 years, from shortly before the outbreak of war until 1961, did sterling work as a supplement to the old suspension bridge, is the focal point of this photo, despite the caption entitled Inverness Castle. "Castle Tolmie", the handsome apartment block on the left of the River Ness's east bank, is still to the fore, though its façade is perhaps a little bit jaded. The splendid limousine in front, almost certainly British-made and coach-built, is tantalisingly too much out of focus to work out the make.*

# FESTIVAL OF NINE LESSONS AND CAROLS

## In THE WEST CHURCH, INVERNESS

on

## THE SUNDAY BEFORE CHRISTMAS, 1951

At 6.30 p.m.

*Organist and Choirmaster: EDWARD N. HALLEY*

ORGAN PRELUDE: Christmas Suite *(Alex. Rowley)*

Intimations

HYMN 69: Once in Royal David's City *(Tune, Irby)*

Prayer and Lord's Prayer

Reception of Offering

CAROL: O Little Town of Bethlehem *(H. Walford Davies)*

FIRST LESSON: Genesis 3, vv. 8-15.  Reader: A Life Boy

God announceth in the Garden of Eden that the seed of woman shall bruise the serpent's head

CAROLS: Silent Night *(Franz Gruber)*

Come, ye lofty *(Geo. J. Elvey)*

SECOND LESSON: Genesis 22, vv. 15-18.  Reader: The Girl Guide Captain

God promiseth to faithful Abraham that in his seed shall all nations of the earth be blessed

CAROL: God rest you merry, gentlemen *(Traditional)*

THIRD LESSON: Isaiah 9, vv. 2, 6, 7.  Reader: A Boys' Brigade Officer

Christ's birth and kingdom are foretold by Esaias

CAROL: A Child this day is born *(Traditional)*

FOURTH LESSON: Isaiah 60, vv. 1-6 and 19.  Reader: A Sunday School Teacher

The prophet in exile foreseeth the glory of the coming of the Lord

CAROL: Jesu, Joy of Man's desiring *(Bach)*

FIFTH LESSON: St. Luke 1, vv. 26-33 and 38.  Reader: The President of the Girls' Association

The angel Gabriel saluteth the blessed Virgin Mary

CAROL: Magnificat *(arr. Edward Bunnett)*

SIXTH LESSON: St. Matthew 1, vv. 18-23.  Reader: A Guildswoman

St. Matthew telleth of Christ's holy birth

PARAPHRASE 37: While humble shepherds watch'd their flocks *(Tune, Winchester)*

SEVENTH LESSON: St. Luke 2, vv. 8-16.  Reader: A Representative of the Choir

The shepherds go unto the manger

CAROL: When the crimson sun had set *(S. S. Greatheed)*

EIGHTH LESSON: St. Matthew 2, vv. 1-11.  Reader: An Elder

The wise men are led by the star to Jesus

CAROLS: We three Kings of Orient are *(J. H. Hopkins)*

O Light of Life *(Bach)*

NINTH LESSON: St. John 1, vv. 1-14.  Reader: The Minister

St. John unfoldeth the mystery of the Incarnation

HYMN 55: O come, all ye faithful *(Tune, Adeste Fideles)*

Prayer

HYMN 46: Hark! the herald angels sing *(Tune, Bethlehem)*

Benediction

ORGAN VOLUNTARY: Grande Offertoire Sur Noël *(Alexandre Guilmant)*

*The varied programme for a Festival of Nine Lessons and Carols held at the West Church, Huntly Street, Inverness, on the Sunday before Christmas 1951. Sadly the Huntly Street building like a number of other River Ness-side churches, has long ceased to be a place of worship, having been converted into a complex of flats about 20 years ago, after the congregation moved to the town's perimeter, at Inshes.*

Boys and leaders of 2nd Ness Bank Company, Boys' Brigade, pictured around 1955.

Members of 2nd Ness Bank Company, Boys' Brigade, of session 1979-80. Can anyone remember what trophy the lads pictured front, right, are holding?

*Former Lord Chancellor Lord Mackay of Clashfern signs the visitors' book at Inverness Town House in the late 1970s, watched by Provost Ian Fraser.*

*Provost Ian Fraser's daughter Vicky is presented to the late Princess Diana, as her proud father looks on. The wee girl of yesteryear now runs the long-established Fraser family funeral directors' firm.*

# Footballers across the decades

Throughout what we might call the modern era, football has developed almost as a religion among many Scottish boys and men, not to mention a small but growing number of women.

Inverness in this respect has been no different from the rest of the country, with dozens of clubs and teams, formal and otherwise, amateur and semi-professional, springing up and fading away across the burgh's decades.

The following pages depict a few of the many teams which vied for goal in bygone days.

*Snapped on Ladies' Walk, on their way to play football at Bught Park, during the war, were these local lads, of whom Joan Clyne, who contributed this photograph, can ider , three: John Mackay, far left, Alec Fridge, third from right and Sandy Junor, second from right. Can any reader identify any of the others?*

Members of Inverness Railway Club team which reached the final of the Scottish Railway Cup in 1980 – rear, from left: J McBean, G Morrison, R MacDonald, L Spence, A MacDonald, G Johnstone, I Mackintosh, G Cormack, J Griffin; front, from left: H Gunning, J McCormack, W Pollock, E Gardiner, G Keir, J Adamiec.

Inverness Railway Club of 1977-78 – rear from left: P Grant, S Waldie, D MacDonald, J McCormack, C Cranford, A Hunter, C Laing, S MacLennan, M McCormick; front, from left: J Innes, W Pollock, M Shewan, H MacDonald, L Thompson, J Mackay, Niall MacLennan (mascot).

*How many still survive from this Inverness Railway Workshop football team pictured at the Bught Park in the early 1950s? The fit young men of yesteryear are – rear, from left: Harry Christie, Jim Sutherland, Jim Calder, Jock Dodds, Billy MacKenzie, Alfie MacDonald; front, from left: Arch MacDonald, Laurie Fraser, Jim Hutcheson, Billy Robertson and Ian MacLeod.*

*Officials and players of Inverness Railway Club football team, taken at the long-demolished Railway Club in the mid-1970s, when they were champions of the Welfare League Division 1. In the picture are, rear, from left: S MacLennan, H MacDonald, M Shewan, J McCormick, G Cormack, H MacDonald, W Pollock, S Waldie; front, from left: C Rennie, A Hunter, C Laing (captain) J Innes, B Sinclair.*

Citadel Football Club's stand and ground at Shore Street Park, some time in the early 20th Century. The club, formed in the mid-1880s was a founder member of the Highland Football League in 1894, though it achieved the honour of league championship only once, in 1909. It left the Highland League in 1935 and staggered on in minor competitions until shortly before World War II. The name was revived in 2008 as a six-a-side team.

Members and officials of Inverness Citadel FC in the early 20th Century. We have no further information of the date or the event. Just visible is the logo of the photographer, Charles Treasurer, whose studio was in Inglis Street.

These fit young lads were members of Inverness Technical High School's Shiel House team, inter-house senior champions in 1955-56. In the photo are, rear, from left: G MacLean, D MacDonald, Mr Gordon, E MacDonald, C MacDougall, A MacKenzie, G Munro; front: N Alakiga, A MacLennan, M Wilson (captain), W Rooney, W Mabon, D Chisholm.

Inverness Thistle FC won a great share of the glory, fielding no less than five team members, when this North of Scotland FA Select beat South of Scotland FA Select 7-2 in September 1955, despite having to undertake the long trek to Stranraer to do so. Its members were, rear, from left: D Mackintosh (reserve), R Lytham (Clach), C Ogilvie (Ross County), J Smith (Caley), F Nimmo, W Hendry (both Thistle), T Irwin (Nairn), T MacNiven (trainer); front: A Grant (Thistle), M Baillie (Caley), R Grant (Thistle), J Mackintosh (Nairn), W Jamieson (Thistle).

*This pre-war photo is of Inverness Caledonian FC Ladies' football team which flourished briefly in the late 1930s, until the outbreak of war sadly put an end to its activities. Does anyone know what the trophy was?*

*Another picture of Inverness Caledonian FC Ladies' football team, which we can date specifically to 14 September 1938, almost a year before its unfortunate demise on the outbreak of war. We know they competed successfully against other ladies' teams from as far afield as Nairn and Elgin. We also know some of their names, rear, from left: Mary Murray, Una Gordon, Betty MacDonald, Ivy Jamieson, Anna Fraser (captain), Lottie MacRae, Tenby Fotheringham, Mrs Riddoch, who washed the team' strips; front: Mairi Munro, Mrs Macdonald?, - Macdonald, - Fraser, Dora MacBean, Mrs Morrison. Do any of these stalwarts still survive?*

This picture shows the lads of Diriebught Thistle with the Youth League Shield, which they won in 1969. They are, rear, from left: Unidentified, Ronald Slucock, unidentified James Grant, Colin White, John MacIver, Charlie Forbes, physical education teacher Colin Baillie; front: Matthew Shaw, Stuart Speed, Robert Bruce, Michael Tuach, Robin Morrison, Hamish Gordon, David Kelman. At that time, the school that is now Millburn Academy was just a small junior secondary unit and in football or rugby only participated in under-13 and under-15 leagues. Hamish Gordon, who contributed the photo, explains: "At that time the under-13 team was pretty good but would not have any competitive fixtures the following season. We decided amongst ourselves to enter the team in the Youth League for the summer prior to the start of the under-15 season, to get some competitive games. I seem to remember that we bought our own tops but used the school's shorts and socks."

Inverness Royal Academy's fifth-year football team, with manager Eddie Hutcheon.

*Members of Queen Street Rovers, Youth League Champions in the early 1970s, pictured with manager John Beaton. They are rear, from left: Ian Hamilton, Peter Wooley, Gordon Gilliespie, John Rae, Ian Clark, unidentified, Roddie MacLennan, Mike Andrew; front: John Robertson, Ian MacGillivray, Kevin MacDonald, Roddy Davidson, unidentified, Mike Godsman.*

*Inaugural Inverness Street League winners of season 1970-71. The young stars in front are, from left: Douglas Lyall, Ronnie Davidson, Kevin MacDonald, pictured with Marion Urquhart, Alex Urquhart, ex-Provost William "Bobo" Mackay and Peggy Mackintosh.*

*Barrel Vault FC, Inverness Welfare League, around 1980. Its members are, rear, from left: Lawrence Spence, Eric Davidson, Gregor MacGregor, Cliff Parr, George Simpson, Dave McKnight, John "Tonto" MacIver; front: Colin "Coco" Gordon, Dunc Munro, Ernie Gardiner, Frank Blinco, Hamish Gordon.*

*From our own old files a picture of a scratch mixed football team made up of employees of Highland News Group of around 20 years ago.*

# Other sports and club activities

*eachkin School hockey team from around 1929 – rear row, from left: Hughina Shaw, Louise MacLennan, Henrietta MacLennan, Annie Robertson, Molly Chisholm, Alice Cameron, Jeannie Stewart; front row, from left: Marion Fraser, Netta Munro, Muriel Webb, Annabel Sinclair, Barbara Cameron. Annie Robertson died in November 2010.*

*Members of Royal Northern Infirmary Badminton Club B League winning team 1964-65, rear, from left: John Pettigrew, Gordon Gillespie, Murdo Smith, Jackie Wilson; front, from left: Mhairi MacKenzie, unidentified, Marjory Smith, Frances Wilson.*

*A photo of ladies of Inverness Golf Club who attended the annual prize-giving ceremony in the early 1970s.*

*Inverness Golf Club prizewinners at the annual prize-giving ceremony in the early 1970s – rear, from left: Hilda Grant, Mary Nicholas, Nessie McGraw, Peg Sutherland unidentified, Maim McClaughlan, Avril Wotherspoon, Beth Fraser, Anne Farquharson, Christine MacDonald; middle, from left: Aileen Fraser, Frances Soutar, Isobel McIntosh Mary Kirk, Janice Cumming; front, from left: Ismay Fraser, Evie Farquhar, Vera Allan, Winnie Gillespie.*

*Inverness Royal Academy basketball team 1982-83, rear, from left: Alasdair Hamilton, unidentified, Brian Robbie, Michael Gillespie, Alan Crawford, Ian Bradley, Brian Reid; front, from left: Brian Shewan, Stewart McEwan, Corran Henderson, Eddie Leighton, John Munro, Sandy MacKenzie, Ivor Robertson.*

*Revellers at the Highland Car Club's annual dinner-dance at the Drumossie Hotel in November 1971. Marjory Dunn, nee MacDonald, who submitted this photo, is third from the left in the front row. Other in the picture include Robbie and Sandra Taylor, Willie and Pat Stewart, Dougie and Linda Riach, Allan Rae, Jim Garden, Nicol and Bev Manson, Campbell and Olive Harper, Norman and Anne Macfarlane.*

*A pause for a souvenir photograph over 60 years ago, when West Church Cycling Club organised an outing to Balloch on 11 July 1939.*

*Inverness lass and cycling enthusiast Tenby Fotheringham snapped on a dykeside by Loch Ness on Sunday, 20 April 1941, during a break in the course of a cycling excursion. Note the white-painted strip on the bicycle mudguard, which along with a reflector substituted for a rear light during the wartime blackout then in force. Ironically, several hundred miles away in Germany, the Great Dictator himself, Adolf Hitler, must have been celebrating his 52nd birthday, while plotting further conquests. Tenby, who died three years ago, is remembered in later life in Inverness for her work with the Scottish Council for Voluntary Services and Age Concern.*

This group of sports prizewinners at Inverness Technical High School in 1953 includes such well known sports personalities of the time as Donald MacKillop, Bob Aitken, Hector Morrison, Nora MacRae, Iris Beaton and possibly two of the "Beauly Triplets". Standing, second from left at the back, is physical education teacher Mr McNab. Marjorie Stuart, who sent this photo in, thinks his first name may have been Edward.

Merkinch Primary School hockey team 1966 – rear, from left: Eileen Wheeler, Eileen Donnachie, Sylvia Clark, Sandra Allan (A), Marie Mackenzie, Glynis Macrae. Front row, from left: Brenda Johnstone, Sandra Allan (B), Eleanor Ross, Mary Murchison, Margaret Wood, Pat Fraser.

*This photo, by the late Sandy McLaren of Star Photos, carries a brief caption on the back, explaining that when Glengarry and Inverness Shinty Clubs met for a friendly match at The Bught Park, Inverness, the Glengarry team mainly used camans made by themselves, as they were finding camans difficult to replace. Referee Ewen MacQueen (left, is seen here examining a pair of Glengarry camans with a couple of Inverness players, but there is no indication of who the two players were, or what they thought of their opponents' equipment.*

*Millburn Secondary School senior rugby Bon-Accord Cup winners 1968-69; rear, from left: Charles Forbes, unidentified, Ian Aird, Jack Gillham, Keith Poole, Charles Sutherland Robert Bruce, Michael Tuach; front: Hamish Gordon, Malcolm Pringle, Alan MacIntosh, James Olsen, John MacIver, unidentified, James Grant.*

*Millburn Secondary School senior seven-a-side rugby, Grant Cup winners 1968/69. Rear, from left: Michael Tuach, Hamish Gordon, Robert Bruce, Charlie Forbes; front: Alan MacIntosh, James Olsen, James Grant.*

*Pictured at Highland Cricket Club's annual dance at Craigmonie Hotel in 1966 were, rear row, from left: Peter Cameron, Len Grant, Alex Munro, Charlie Massie, Kenny Urquhart; middle row: Rhoda Cameron, Christine Grant, Pat Watson, Alan Watson, Billy Macpherson, Charlie Palmer, Isobel Urquhart, Duncan Mackay; front: Tom MacNiven, Kenny Burke, Eddie Pawson, Rosemary Pawson, Liz Massey, Bobby Robertson, Sheila Mackintosh, Willie John Mackintosh and Pat Mackay.*

*Prizewinners of Inverness and District Badminton Club at the annual prizegiving in the Palace Hotel, 1975. The veteran in the middle is the late Chris Mackay, who gave a great deal of his spare time over many years to coaching young badminton players, with little public recognition. He seems to be receiving a presentation watch.*

*Prizewinners of Inverness & District Badminton Friendly League photographed at the Palace Hotel in 1975.*

An Inverness Badminton Club team who played their counterparts in Stornoway in 1972. They are, rear, from left: Donnie MacDonald, unidentified, Andrew Murdoch, Peter MacCutheon, Davd Munro; front: Liz Anderson, Marlene MacLean, Helen Godfrey, Annette Burnett, Bonnie Cruickshank, Peg MacDonald.

# MACLEOD'S CARAVANS

- THE FAMILY BUSINESS WITH OVER 41 YRS EXPERIENCE
- LARGE RANGE OF NEW & USED STATIC & TOURING CARAVANS
- PART EXCHANGE WELCOME

## OPEN 6 DAYS
## AND SUNDAY BY APPOINTMENT

- FINANCE AVAILABLE (WRITTEN DETAILS ON REQUEST)
- DON'T HESITATE PHONE JANE OR STEVEN NOW!
- VISIT OUR SHOP, LARGE RANGE OF ACCESSORIES

### EVANTON

## (01349) 830632

### Fax (05601) 162422

Email: janemacpherson@btconnect.com

## www.macleodscaravans.co.uk

---

# LOOKING FOR A QUALITY USED VOLVO?

## IAN CATTANACH CAR SALES

### 13 Carsegate Road, Inverness IV3 8EX

## Tel: 01463 717200
## Mobile: 07713 642892

## www.usedvolvocars.com

---

# DUNCAN FRASER
## (FISHMONGER)

*Established 1927*
*84 Years*

**For all occasions try our vast and varied selection of fresh local fish and seafood.**

*Large selection available from Seabass to Salmon*

**Telephone 01463 232744**
8-10 QUEENSGATE ARCADE, INVERNESS

---

# THE GELLIONS HOTEL

*The Inverness pub with a long tradition of real Highland hospitality*

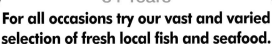

William McGonagall (1825-1902) has been described as the very best of the world's worst poets! In 1894 Mr A. Gossip invited McGonagall to Inverness...

GELLION'S HOTEL
INVERNESS, *October 14th 1894.*

Most Miraculous Minstrel,

As chairman of the "Heather Blend Club," I am directed by the members of that august body to solicit the honour of your patronage and presence at our annual dinner, which takes place at the above hotel on the evening of the 18th inst. You are requested to come in Highland costume, and in case your accoutrements are in need to some alight repairs, I enclose you five shillings in stamps. This sum will in no way prejudice the silvery collection your will receive here in person.

Your appearance on the Inverness platform, by the train leaving Perth at 10 a.m., will be sufficient acceptance of this cordial invitation. – Your truly,
A. Gossip
P.S. – Show this letter to the authorities at Perth Station, and it will pass you to Inverness and back.
A. G.

**The great poet was met at Inverness Station and describes his visit to the Gellions Hotel...**

He was a tall, powerful, handsome man, whose genial manners and perfect courtesy at once put me perfectly at ease. He escorted me to the hotel, where he introduced me to the landlord, who told me in a very hearty way to order what I liked, and when I liked, as long as I stayed at his hotel. As I was hungry, I took full advantage of this carte blanche, and ordered and dispatched to two cups of coffee the largest, thickest and best beef steak I ever saw, even in dreams.

Two hours after this dinner was served, and the members (a goodly crew) as well as myself did ample justice to the good things provided.

*Follow in the steps of the poet . . . enjoy the atmosphere of the Highland Capital's favourite pub*
## GOOD FOOD • REAL ALES • OPEN ALL DAY – ALL WEEK

# BRIDGE STREET, INVERNESS, Tel. (01463) 236558

**DUNCANS**
digital solutions centre

▶ Service Agent for Sony, Panasonic, JVC, Sanyo, Samsung

▶ Sales & RepairsSpecialist
▶ Aerials Supplied & Installed
▶ Satellite Systems
▶ Plasma & LCD Specialist
▶ Home Cinema Systems
▶ TV Wall Mounting Service

# tel: 01463 712151

Showroom ▶ 11 Carsegate Road, Inverness

# THE DRAWING ROOM
...for beautiful gifts

rosie brown

*Sheila Fleet*

Open Mon-Sat 10am-6pm

14 Kingsmills Road, Crown, Inverness Tel: 01463 711888

## www.drawingroomgifts.com

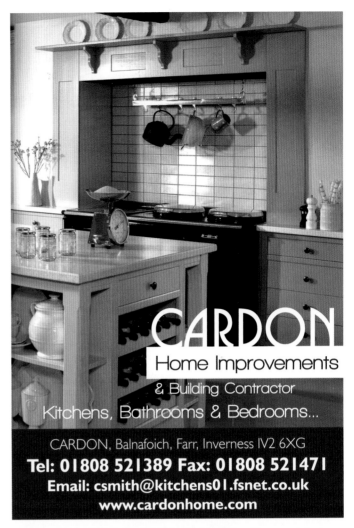

# CARDON
## Home Improvements
### & Building Contractor
## Kitchens, Bathrooms & Bedrooms...

CARDON, Balnafoich, Farr, Inverness IV2 6XG
**Tel: 01808 521389 Fax: 01808 521471**
Email: csmith@kitchens01.fsnet.co.uk
**www.cardonhome.com**

Calterdon

BMW
The Ultimate Driving Machine

**Calterdon**
Harbour Road, Inverness IV1 1UA
Tel: 01463 236566 **www.calterdonbmw.co.uk**

**Established in 1971**

# CHARLIE'S CAFE

*An Inverness tradition since 1952*

## Last stop before the Bus Stop
## A place to meet, a place to eat
### All Day Breakfast
### Home Cooking
### Daily Specials

*Modern facilities including:*

Air conditioning

Disabled facilities • Open kitchen

**2 Margaret Street, Farraline Park
Bus Station, Inverness**

## 01463 233498

Open 8am-7pm Monday – Saturday

10am-6pm Sunday

EAT safe

---

**Wiltshire Farm Foods**

*delicious meals to your door*

*Where people care about food – and you*

- Choose from over 300 mouth-watering meals and deserts
- From as little as £2.25 for a main meal and vegetables
- Special diets and allergies catered for
- Easy to order • Friendly reliable service

Call us for your Free Brochure

## 01466 799620

or order online at www.wiltshirefarmfoods.com

*Rizza's* of Huntly

---

## Inverness Autospray
### Panelbeating – Spray Paint Specialists

Proprietor: Mike Sturrock, Unit 10-4 Carsegate Road South, INVERNESS IV3 8LL Tel: 01463 229677 Email: mikesturrock@btopenworld.com

---

## German build quality ◆ Italian design flair ◆ Made in Scotland

## Metris® at AshleyAnn▲▲

18 Carsegate Rd, Inverness. T: 01463 711548. E: inverness@ashleyann.co.uk

# www.ashleyann.co.uk

# MORAY FIRTH BLINDS

- *FREE, no obligation quote*
- *FREE fitting*
- *Serving all of the Highlands*
- *Made to measure service*

Manufacturer of child friendly senses rollers
Standard rollers, verticals and perfect fit.
We also supply all types of Venetian, Pleated, Velux, Intu, Roman and Curtains

Choose in the comfort of your home
or visit our showroom at
26 Millbank Road, Munlochy, Ross-shire

**01463 811274**

## CASTLE
### RESTAURANT

CASTLE STREET • INVERNESS • TEL: (01463) 230925
**Family Run Business**
• Catering for the Highlands for 52 years •
The good food people for 3 Qs
QUALITY  QUANTITY  QUICKNESS
Open for Breakfast, Morning Coffees,
Lunches and Evening Meals. Carry out meals available.
Served from 9am-8.30pm • Closed Sundays

# SAMARITANS

## INVERNESS

# 24/7 EMOTIONAL SUPPORT

# 01463 713456
# 08457 909090

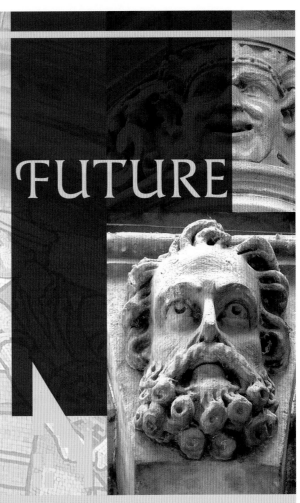

# INVERNESS
## CITY HERITAGE TRUST

# Taking the PAST into the FUTURE

The built heritage is crucial to the well being of our community, our tourism industry and in attracting economic investment to the centre of Inverness. We want the Inverness City Heritage Trust to stimulate a dynamic urban environment where traditional and contemporary co-exist: a confident and creative Inverness, where cultural heritage is appreciated and enjoyed by locals and visitors alike.

Inverness City Heritage Trust is an independent charitable company limited by guarantee.  The Trust's main aim is to take a strategic view of the repair and maintenance needs of the buildings forming the historic core of the city and to co-ordinate a programme of conservation work funded by grant assistance in the Riverside and Crown Conservation Areas. It also gives advice to building owners, produces publications and helps to organise events and exhibitions for people interested in the history of buildings and architecture in Inverness.

For more info call: 01463 724384 or visit the website at
www.heritage-inverness.org

## Think Karndean, Amtico or Quickstep

### ...THINK SHARON LEON HOME FLOORINGS!

**SharonLeon**
Home Floorings

33 Harbour Road, Inverness IV1 1UA Scotland
Email: sales@sharonleoncarpets.co.uk
*Established 1963*

Call us now on
**01463 234079**
sharonleoncarpets.co.uk

✔ **See our amazing displays instore**
✔ **Massive choice held in stock**
✔ **Luxury Vinyl and Wooden floors**

---

## MORAY FIRTH TRAINING
*'where quality counts'*
### Established 1966

**APPROVED FIRST AID AT WORK TRAINING**
Emergency, Certificate and Requalification Courses
(held regularly in our Training Centre or on site if required)

Training and Management of Motor Vehicle Apprentices to National Vocational Qualification standards.

Other courses:
Manual Handling (Kinetic Techniques)
Abrasive Wheels

*For further details contact us at:*
**32 HARBOUR ROAD, INVERNESS**
**Tel: 01463 230036    Fax: 01463 712829**
**Email: moray.firth.trg@cali.co.uk**
**www.mftg.co.uk**

---

*William Morrison*
Watchmaker & Jeweller at Finkelstein
*Established 1902 by Isaac Finkelstein*

Quality Traditional
and Antique Style
Jewellery
& Gifts

18 Market Arcade
Inverness IV1 1PG

Tel/Fax: 01463 221710

---

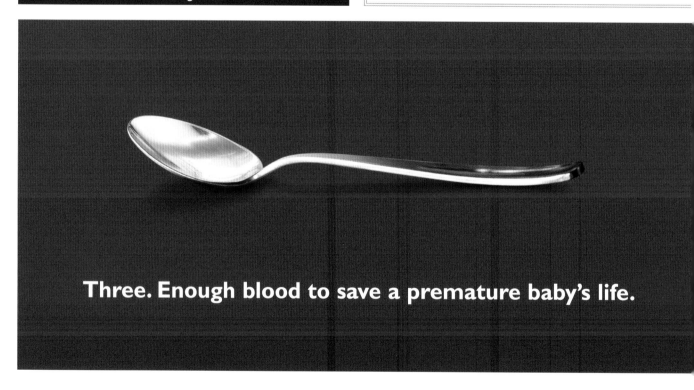

## Three. Enough blood to save a premature baby's life.

### To register as a blood donor or to find a session near you
### call 0845 30 17 2 70 or visit us at www.scotblood.co.uk

**NHS**
National
Services
Scotland

## Highland Photographic Archive
### Home to a wealth of local images spanning a century or more

## Inverness Museum and Art Gallery
### Come and visit this exciting and interactive museum in the centre of Inverness

**Inverness Museum & Art Gallery**
**Castle Wynd, Inverness.  Tel: 01463 237114**
 E: Inverness.Museum@highlifehighland. com
**Photographic Archive**
 E: Photographic.Archive@highlifehighland.com
 www.inverness.highland.museum

high**life**
highland
na gàidhealtachd

**Opening hours:**

**1st April - 31st October**
　　　　　Tuesday - Saturday　10am –5pm

**1st November - 31st March**
　　　　　Thursday - Saturday　10am—5pm

# TOMATIN

ESTᴰ 1897

── SINGLE MALT ──

HIGHLAND SCOTCH WHISKY

*5 men, 177 years of pride and passion*

*Embrace the Spirit of the Highlands*

Martin Hendry
Head Mashman

Richard Noble
Warehouse Manager

Robert Nixon
Head Stillman

Iain Duthie
Head Cooper

Douglas Campbell
Master Distiller

THE TOMATIN DISTILLERY Co. LTD

SCOTCH MALT WHISKY DISTILLERS

THE BRANDS

TOMATIN, THE ANTIQUARY, BIG"T" & THE TALISMAN

www.tomatin.com

PLEASE SAVOUR RESPONSIBLY www.drinkaware.co.uk

## Worry-free means all this is included:

- A new scooter or powered wheelchair every three years
- Standard pricing nationwide
- Insurance
- Breakdown assistance
- Servicing,
- maintenance and repairs
- Tyre and battery replacement
- A dedicated UK based Customer Service team
- Reliability and peace of mind

**Motability**
www.motability.co.uk

Find out if you're eligible to get a Motability scooter or powered wheelchair by calling 0800 953 3060

*City*

**M♿BILITY**

46a Seafield Road
Longman Industrial Estate
Inverness IV1 1SG
Tel: **01463 250850** Fax: **01463 250950**
email: **info@city-mobility.co.uk**
*Covering the North of Scotland*

# WOODY'S
*World Famous*
## SNACK BAR
At the INVERNESS TRUCK STOP
## BUFFETS by CATERING FIRST

### The Lorry Park at 12 Henderson Road Inverness

## LUNCHES • BREAKFASTS
## HOT & COLD ROLLS
## HOT & COLD DRINKS

### Delivered throughout the day till 2pm
~ *Free Delivery on orders over £5* ~

- Why not have Sunday morning breakfast & newspaper delivered to your door
- Diabetic & Vegetarian Palates catered for

## Telephone
# 01463 710711 / 715815

# CAMERONS
## BARBER SHOP
### — THE —
# GENTLEMANS
## BARBER

### The perfect cut every time, no need to book, simply call in to

**101 Academy Street,
Inverness
Tel. 01463 710111**

www.ambaile.org.uk

**am baile**

*Explore Am Baile*

The Highland Council's award winning bilingual heritage and culture website and find out more about the history and culture of Inverness

The Highland Council
Comhairle na Gàidhealtachd

Supported by
BIG LOTTERY FUND

*Am Baile is managed as part of Highland Libraries*

# THE Music Station

*Celebrating 30 years in business • Established October 1981*

**49 CHURCH STREET • INVERNESS IV1 1DR**
Tel: 01463 225523 • Fax: 01463 718900
sales@the-music-station.co.uk
www.the-music-station.co.uk

## Supply, Service, Installation & Repairs to our AUDIO Customers

*Leading Brands:*

Fender  BLACK★  Marshall  YAMAHA  Peavey  Ibanez  BOSE  sch guitar  SONOS Announcing the Sonos Wireless Dock

---

# The DORES INN

The DORES INN, Loch Ness,
Inverness, IV2 6TR. Tel 01463 751203
Only 10 minutes from Inverness

Come and enjoy the breathtaking views of the loch and then enjoy a glass of wine or one of our real ales in the pub.

Our fantastic restaurant opens at 10am daily serving breakfasts, coffee and home baking, our lunch menu starts at noon followed by dinner until late.

*We look forward to welcoming you soon.*

The STOREHOUSE

Visit our sister restaurant at Foulis
**The STOREHOUSE Restaurant & Farm Shop**
Foulis Ferry, Evanton IV16 9UX
Tel: 01349 830038

---

# HIGHLAND WINDSCREEN SERVICES

## CAR   VAN   HGV
## PLANT   BUS/COACH

www.highlandwindscreenservices.co.uk

- **WINDSCREENS**
- **BODY GLASS**
- **STONE CHIP REPAIRS**
- **AIR-CON RECHARGE/MAINTENANCE**
- **VAN CONVERSIONS**
- **PROFURB WHEEL REFURBS**
- **INSURANCE DIRECT BILLING**
- **WINDOW TINTING**

 ata AUTOMOTIVE TECHNICIAN ACCREDITATION
 SVQ
AGENTS FOR
 NATIONWIDE WINDSCREEN

# www.highlandwindscreenservices.co.uk
**Unit 10 Carsegate Road South, Inverness IV3 8LL**
email: mail@highlandwindscreenservices.co.uk
Tel: **01463 710940**  Mob: **07879 477165**  Fax: **01463 710367**